MADE
IN TEXAS

Also by Michael Lind:

The Next American Nation: The New Nationalism and the Fourth American Revolution (1995)

Up From Conservatism: Why the Right is Wrong for America (1996)

Powertown (1996)

The Alamo: An Epic (1997)

Hamilton's Republic: Readings in the American Democratic Nationalist Tradition (1997)

Vietnam, the Necessary War: A Reinterpretation of America's Most Disastrous Military Conflict (1999)

The Radical Center: The Future of American Politics (2001)

Bluebonnet Girl (2003)

MADE
IN TEXAS

George W. Bush
and the Southern Takeover
Of American Politics

MICHAEL LIND

BASIC
BOOKS

NEW
AMERICA
BOOKS

A New America Book, Published by Basic Books,
A Member of the Perseus Books Group

Designed by Bookcomp, Inc.

A CIP catalog record for this book is available from the Library of Congress.

ISBN 0-465-04121-3
03 04 05 / 10 9 8 7 6 5 4 3 2 1

In memory of
Decherd Turner
(1922–2002)
valiant for truth

CONTENTS

CONTENTS

INTRODUCTION

Between 1964 and 2000, the state of Texas was home to three elected presidents (Lyndon Johnson, George H. W. Bush, and George W. Bush), two vice-presidential candidates (George H. W. Bush and Lloyd Bentsen), and one independent presidential candidate (H. Ross Perot), who in 1992 received 19 percent of the vote—more than any third-party candidate since Theodore Roosevelt in 1912. The Lone Star State, having long been known for its exports of cotton, oil, and cattle, was now exporting presidents and would-be presidents.

Other states have produced presidential dynasties. There was a Virginia dynasty in the early 1800s, and an Ohio dynasty in the late nineteenth century, followed by a California dynasty made up of Nixon and Reagan. But the presidents belonging to other political dynasties from a single state tended to belong to the same party and to share a common outlook; the Virginia presidents believed in states' rights, the Ohio presidents favored industrial tariffs, the California presidents were vigorous anti-communists in foreign policy. The Texans, however, have been not only remarkably diverse but also incompatible—and in some cases, mutually hostile. In less than three decades, Texas gave the country the most liberal president in American history—and two of the most conservative. Ignore Lyndon Johnson for a moment; George H. W. Bush and Ross Perot—whose independent presidential bid probably cost the elder Bush the election in 1992—might as well have been from different states, if not different countries, so dissimilar were their values and programs. In 1992, Americans in other parts of the country along with foreign observers could have been forgiven for thinking that a civil war in Texas had spilled over into national politics.

It had. There is indeed a civil war in Texas, and it has been going on for generations. The division between the rival forces does not correspond to a simple left/right dichotomy. Lyndon Johnson and Ross Perot have been on one side, and the Tory Democrat Lloyd Bentsen along with the Republican Bushes have been on the other.

The two sides in this old and continuing struggle can be described as the Texan traditionalists and the Texan modernists. The traditionalists are content for Texas to have a low-wage, low-tax, commodity-exporting economy—even if the result is a society with enormous inequalities of wealth and opportunity. The modernists treasure the good aspects of the rural folk heritage of Texas as much as the traditionalists do, and their military-tinged patriotism is, if anything, even deeper. But the Texan modernists have had a radically different vision of what Texas, and, by implication, what America should be: a high-tech economy with a meritocratic society. If traditionalist Texas is symbolized by oil companies, ranches, and farms, modernist Texas is symbolized by the Johnson Space Center in Houston and the computer industry that grew up in the late twentieth century in Austin's "Silicon Hills."

From the 1960s until the present, the conservative traditionalists—led in national politics by the two Bushes and Republican congressional leaders like Senator Phil Gramm and Representatives Tom DeLay and Dick Armey—have displaced the modernists in Texas, whose power peaked in the 1950s when Sam Rayburn controlled the House and Lyndon Johnson controlled the Senate. As this suggests, the rise of the traditionalist right and the decline of the New Deal since the 1960s have been at one and the same time a trend in Texas and a national phenomenon.

While the Texan modernist tradition, like the broader New Deal tradition of which it was a part, has been marginalized, even in Texas itself, the reactionary conservatism of the Texan traditionalists has grown in confidence and political influence. Indeed, it is no exaggeration to speak of the "Texanization" of the American right as a whole. From William F. Buckley, Jr., the son of a Texas oil man, to those two other Texas oil men, George H. W. Bush and George W. Bush, conservative thinkers and politicians rooted in the old Texan commodity-exporting oligarchy have redefined what conservatism means in the United States. Even in the Northeast and Midwest, older, rival conservative traditions—the conservative progressivism of the New Englanders, the isolationist and protectionist conservatism of the Midwest—have been replaced by a recognizably Texan (and broadly Southern) conservatism that unites a belief in minimal government at home and a bellicose foreign policy abroad with religious fundamentalism.

Although they influenced the administrations of Reagan and the elder Bush, as well as the House of Representatives after the Republican takeover in 1994, it was not until George W. Bush became president and the vast machinery of the executive branch was in their hands that the Texan traditionalists and their allies had the power to shape national policy. The result was not just a conservative administration, but a conservative Texan administration. In domestic policy, any conservative president would have been solicitous of the interests of business, but the Bush–Cheney energy plan, like its environmental policy, reflected the agenda of the Texas oil patch in which the biggest player was Enron, whose bankruptcy shattered confidence in the U.S. economy in 2002. Bush's foreign policy was made in Texas, too. In the first two years of his administration, Bush alienated America's closest allies with a reflexive unilateralism influenced by Texan traditions of militarism and a policy of uncritical support for right-wing nationalists in Israel influenced by the Protestant religious right in Texas and other states of the American South.

The fact that a product of traditional Texan conservatism was in the White House at the beginning of the twenty-first century, then, had profound implications for both the United States and the world. To a degree that has not been the case since the mid-twentieth century, when Lyndon Johnson led the Senate and Sam Rayburn led the House, national politics and Texan politics are intertwined. How and why the same state, within a few decades, has exported radically different political philosophies and programs to the rest of America and the world is the subject of this book.

The story I tell is necessarily one of "dead white males." Until the 1960s, Texas was a rigidly segregated Southern state with a gender code based on age-old notions of masculine and feminine honor. The

battles over politics and policy in Texas were almost exclusively strug-
gles among white male Southerners of British Protestant descent.
Since the Civil Rights Revolution, black and Latino Texans have
helped to transform the politics and culture of Texas, even as immigration has transformed its demography. This is a story that deserves
to be told—but it is not the story I tell in this book.

The political history of Texas and its implications for America and
the world is a topic of more than scholarly interest to me. A fifth-
generation Texan, I was born, raised, and educated in Texas and never
lived outside of the state until I studied foreign policy in graduate
school at Yale in the 1980s. I have to go back three generations, to my
great-grandparents, to find ancestors who were not born and buried
inside the borders of the Lone Star State.

One of my ancestors who migrated to Texas was a native of Connecticut who married into a Virginia planter family but was driven
from Virginia to Texas because of his abolitionist views, while a distant collateral relative, a Confederate slaveowner, had his farm in
Georgia burned by General Sherman's army. Another ancestor of
mine, a German immigrant, Joseph Goodman, who according to family tradition was Jewish, showed up in Austin following the Civil War
in the Federal army of occupation of General George Armstrong
Custer, in which he had been a hostler (horse handler). The Goodman Building, the store he owned next to the state capitol in Austin,
with a deed signed by Sam Houston, is now a historic monument.

On my mother's side, my ancestors were largely Scottish, Scots-
Irish, and Anglo-American pioneers, who migrated westward from Virginia, where the first of them arrived in the 1620s, along the
Appalachian and Ozark mountains to Texas. My great-grandfather, the
first acting dean of Southern Methodist University, educated at the
University of Wisconsin, grew up on a farm in Arkansas. His father,
crippled when a train hit the carriage he was driving, had been forced
to make soap for his neighbors in order to support his family; his sons
took turns working on the farm in order to put one another through
college. One of them, my Great-Great-Uncle Jasper, became a
Methodist circuit preacher in Arkansas and Texas known for the sever-

ity of his views. By way of my mother's family, I am a distant cousin of Larry Hagman, who portrayed the archetypal Texan wheeler-dealer J. R. Ewing on the 1980s soap opera *Dallas,* as well as a distant nephew of his mother, the actress Mary Martin, a native of Weatherford, Texas.

My father's family consisted of Swedish peasants who immigrated during the Scandinavian famines of the 1870s and 1880s to East-Central Texas, where they picked cotton until they could afford small farms of their own. In the early twentieth century, from the family farm on the prairie, my Swedish-American grandmother remembered seeing, in the distance, a bonfire of the Ku Klux Klan. The Swedish farmers were not liberals, but they lacked the violent racial prejudices of their Southern neighbors. My Swedish great-grandfather gave black neighbors permission to build a church called the Blue Goose on his farm, and, around World War I, would sit in his rocking chair on the porch, listening to the sermons and the songs.*

My paternal grandfather worked during the Depression as a janitor sweeping the floors of the student union building at the University of Texas, where he listened to the impromptu talks of a young man who, he told my grandmother, would be important someday: the young John Connally. The first of his family to receive a college education, thanks to the GI Bill, my father in his 20s was elected county attorney of Blanco County, Lyndon Johnson's home county. My mother's most vivid memory of LBJ is of his annoyance when, at a county picnic, my mother served Lady Bird before she served him. As a young lawyer in Austin, my father met Frank Hamer, the legendary Texas Ranger who had shot and killed the bank robbers Bonnie and Clyde. When drinking at the Driskill Hotel in downtown Austin, Hamer was always careful to sit where he had an exit nearby and a view of all entrances. Perhaps he had in mind the fate of Ben Thompson, the gunslinger whom the city of Austin hired as marshall, before he was gunned down at San Antonio's Vaudeville Theater in 1884.

---

*Perhaps the black congregation assumed that their church would be safe on his property. The name "Blue Goose" seems to have been a reference to a road in the vicinity.

Growing up in Austin, the state capital, where my father became an assistant attorney general, I knew the attorney general and the mayor as visitors to my parents' house. One of George W. Bush's White House aides, the son of a family friend, as a child wore hand-me-down clothes that I had outgrown. My aunt by marriage, the novelist Shelby Hearon, assisted Barbara Jordan when she wrote her memoirs. At the other end of the political spectrum, the son of Martin Dies, the red-baiting Texan congressman who was the head of the House Un-American Activities Committee, was a family acquaintance. My own experience in politics included working during college for a liberal Democrat in the State Senate—where one of my tasks was to pick up new laws from a lobbyist whom I would meet in various dimly lit, smoky saloons—and heading the neoconservative Federalist Society at the University of Texas Law School.

My background, of course, is no warrant for the truth of my views. But personal experience and family tradition, along with political lore passed down by friends and acquaintances but never committed to paper, give me an advantage over other scholars in sifting fact from fiction in controversies about the past in Texas. If I was not there, I know a lot of people who were, or who were told what happened by their predecessors.*

Although I was fortunate enough to grow up in a middle-class suburb, in my youth I knew and often worked with members of the majority of Texans, including many of my relatives, who belong to the working class: impoverished white "cedar-choppers" in the hills west of Austin, Mexican-Americans whose families arrived in different waves of immigration between the nineteenth century and the present, black Americans only a few generations removed from slavery and only one generation removed from segregation. One of my paternal grandmother's neighbors in East Austin, the late Horace Fowler,

---

*For example, when I read Robert Caro's biography of Lyndon Johnson, I asked my father, who was fairly conservative, what he thought of Caro's claim that Coke Stevenson was a noble, tragic figure. "*Coke Stevenson?*" my father replied in disbelief. "Oh, hell, he was a tool of the oil companies."

mowed lawns for a living in order to support his vocation as a preacher to inmates in prisons throughout Texas. A saying of his has always stayed with me: "Tell the truth and spite the Devil." Although my Devil, unlike his, is a symbol, telling the truth to spite the Devil is the purpose of this book.

ONE

A Tale of Two Ranches

Two presidents; two ranches.

When Lyndon Johnson was president of the United States between 1963 and 1969, the world grew familiar with the "Western White House"—the Johnson ranch on the Pedernales River west of the state capital of Austin. Following his election in 2000, President George W. Bush has hosted foreign leaders and American officials at his own ranch north of Austin in Crawford, Texas. To make sure that the television audience got the point, Bush aides hung a pompous "Western White House" seal at the Crawford elementary school when briefings were held there. The two presidential ranches may seem similar. But they and their surroundings differ in profound ways, providing significant clues to the political traditions and cultural values associated with two very different presidents from Texas.*

George W. Bush was ridiculed in the liberal press as a phony rancher, and indeed many of his activities on the ranch, like ostentatiously clearing brush in the heat of midsummer or signing bills in front of neighbors seated on hay bales, were publicity stunts. But that George W. Bush was an authentic cultural Texan, there could be no doubt. Although born in New Haven, Connecticut, the grandson of a U.S. senator from Connecticut and the son of an immigrant from the Northeast

---

*During his tenure in the White House, George H. W. Bush spent his vacations at the family home in Kennebunkport, Maine. The elder Bush's "home" in Texas consisted of a hotel suite in Houston, which the hotel rented out in his absence. Following his defeat in his reelection bid in 1992, the elder Bush retired to West Oaks, an exclusive neighborhood of Houston.

whose heart always remained in Kennebunkport, Maine, George W. Bush grew up in West Texas and absorbed the folk culture of Texas along with the worldview of members of the native white Protestant Texan elite.

In 1969, when George W. Bush was 23 years old, the historian D. W. Meinig described the West Texas in which he had grown up from the age of 3. With the exception of a tiny number of blacks and Mexican-Americans, Meinig wrote,

> the population of the region is perhaps the purest example of the "native white Anglo-Saxon Protestant" culture in Texas. And it is such in the popular mind as well as in historical fact; a recent local writer on religion noted that the leaders of the largest church in his city took great pride in the fact that the South Plains was settled by a "pure blooded, homogeneous popula- tion . . . from the great Anglo-Saxon centers of the South." . . . Emancipated from the narrowest folk expressions of Southern fundamentalism, it remains thoroughly within and indeed gives much leadership to the mainstream of Southern Protestant development, with Baptists and Methodists dominant, and the Disciples of Christ, the Church of Christ, and various other evan- gelical sects prominent. . . . The undiluted Southern background has made it a routinely segregationist society. In the past the Ku Klux Klan found strong support and in various localities there have been attempts to keep Negroes out or to drive away those few who have drifted in.

Of West Texas political culture in 1969, Meinig wrote: "On the whole West Texas is a strongly conservative political area, with a form of conservatism . . . [that blends] the provincial, rural, folk conser- vatism of the native Texan-Southern tradition with the strongly ideo- logical economic conservatism of the newer wealthy class of the Southwest and West. Put in 1964 terms, it was a region with many Goldwater Democrats."[1] Barry Goldwater carried, besides his own Arizona, only a few Deep South states—more or less the same states carried by Strom Thurmond's segregationist candidacy in 1948 and George Wallace's racist American Party in 1968. A product of a sec- tion of Texas that never forgave Johnson for his championship of civil rights for black Americans, George W. Bush grew up in what may very well have been, apart from black-belt counties in Alabama, Mississippi, Georgia, and South Carolina, the most reactionary community in English-speaking North America.

One typical example of the West Texas political culture that produced the two Bushes was J. Evetts Haley, a rancher active in conservative politics for almost half a century. In the 1930s, he belonged to the Jeffersonian Democrats, an anti-Roosevelt organization funded by right-wing businessmen. Among other things, Haley accused FDR of allowing Catholics into the Postal Service "to wipe out Protestantism." He ran for the Democratic nomination for governor on a segregationist platform in 1956, while crusading against liberal professors.[2] In his 1964 book, *A Texan Looks at Lyndon*, a conspiracy-theory tract that found an enthusiastic readership among members of the John Birch Society and others on the far right, Haley warned that Johnson's statement "that man's best hope lies in the realm of reason" proved that Johnson had "humanist leanings." The Civil Rights Act of 1964, Haley predicted, would bring about the end of the American Republic.

————————

The Bush ranch in Crawford is far in miles—although not in spirit—from the West Texas where George W. Bush spent his childhood. Although Bush was a newcomer to the area, in terms of politics the region was Bush country. The white voters of McLennan County, although not its numerous black and Latino residents, were among the strongest supporters of Bush in both his gubernatorial and presidential campaigns. What is more, since the years before the Civil War, McLennan County has been identified with the intense economic, racial, and religious conservatism of yesterday's Southern Democrats who are the political and sometimes lineal ancestors of today's Southern Republicans.

Eighteen miles from Crawford is Waco, Texas. Roughly seventy miles south of Dallas, Waco is located in central McLennan County, near the juncture of the Brazos and Bosque rivers. One of contemporary Waco's tourist attractions, not far from the Bush ranch, is the Texas Rangers Hall of Fame. Most of the famous incidents involving the Texas Rangers took place in South Texas and along the Texas border with Mexico. But there is a reason why the Texas Rangers museum is located in East Texas, rather than in South Texas. Many Mexican-Texans and Mexicans hated and feared *los rincheros*, whom they considered to be racist thugs and murderers enforcing the racial caste system and monopoly over power and profit of Anglo-Texans. A Texas Rangers Hall of Fame in a border town——Laredo, say, or El Paso—would be the equivalent of a memorial to the Confederate cavalry in a black neighborhood or a shrine to the Cossacks in a Jewish neighborhood. The attempts of the city of Waco to associate itself with the Western frontier, like the Western imagery of Bush's ranch, should fool no one. Waco and Crawford are not in the West, but in the Deep South.

Waco, like Austin and Dallas, is built along the Balcones fault, a long crack in the crust curving northeastward through Texas that was created when the Great Plains and the Rockies rose millions of years ago. In each case, settlers were attracted to the site of a future city because a river that descended from higher country in the west—the Lower Colorado (Austin), the Brazos (Waco), and the Trinity (Dallas)—provided springs for drinking water and waterfalls for mills, and, later, dams.[3] The land to the east of the Balcones fault, flat and enriched by detritus from aeons of erosion in the hills and plateaus to the west, has rich black soil. Beginning in the 1840s, Southerners established cotton plantations along the fertile Brazos and Colorado river bottoms. As a result, well into the twentieth century, Waco was a center of cotton production and marketing. During the Civil War, the Confederacy produced cotton cloth at Barron's Mill. At the beginning of the twentieth century, one of the largest cotton mills in the South, Kirksey Woolen Mills, was located in Waco. By 1900, Waco was literally the center of the cotton world: the United States led the world in cotton production, Texas produced more cotton than the other Southern states, and the northern Brazos Valley was the leading cotton region in Texas.[4] In 1909, Waco built a gaudy Cotton Palace for festivals.

Nearby Crawford took part in the regional economy; in 1890, it had its own cotton gin, and its major products were cotton, corn, wheat, and cowhides. While the mill owners and other affluent Waco citizens lived in ornate mansions in a neighborhood with the elegant name of Provident Heights, poor white and black mill workers lived in Dickensian conditions in a neighborhood with the inelegant name of Edgefield.

Few Texans were as enthusiastic about the secession of the South from the United States as the white inhabitants of Waco. Six Confederate generals were Waco residents, and the Confederate States of America (CSA) raised seventeen companies from Waco and surrounding towns like Crawford. The most important political figure whom Texas produced was Richard Coke (1829–1897), who fought in the Confederate Army and was elected governor in 1873, after the administration of Grant abandoned Texas to him and other ex-Confederate politicians. Under Coke's leadership, the Democrats of Texas, united behind the cause of white supremacy, regained power in the state government, imposed strict racial segregation, and created the one-party system by which the Democrats ruled the state until the Civil Rights Revolution in the 1950s and 1960s. Elected to the United States Senate in 1873, Coke made further contributions to the cause of white supremacy by voting against the Force Bill, a precursor of the Voting Rights Act of 1965, which would have provided federal protection for citizens intimidated by violence from voting; he also voted against federal aid to public schools. The segregationist anti-Roosevelt Democrat Coke Stevenson (1888–1975), the governor of Texas from 1941 to 1947, was named after him.

Although there were Catholic, Methodist, and black Protestant colleges in Waco, the city was dominated by Baylor University, a college owned by the Baptist General Convention of Texas. Today Baylor claims to be the largest Baptist university in the world. In 1886, the institution, previously known as Waco University, was named after the founder of an earlier version of the school in Independence, Texas, Judge R. E. B. Baylor. Baylor University quickly became—and remains—a center of Protestant fundamentalism, with a gravitational influence that has drawn wilder Christian cults to its environs.

Despite the suspicion of Greek philosophy shared by many evangelical Protestants, Waco over the years has taken pride in its nickname, "the Athens of Texas." Residents of more liberal Austin, a few hundred miles to the south, had other names for it in the late twentieth century: "Wacko" and "Jerusalem on the Brazos." The anti-intellectual culture of the Waco fundamentalists made the city what H. L. Mencken said the South as a whole was: a "Sahara of the Bozart." During the 1970s, some Waco Christians sought to detect coded Satanic messages in rock music records by playing them backward. Diabolical LPs and books were burned in public bonfires by the local ayatollahs of this American version of Iran's Holy City of Qum or the Florence of Savonarola.

The only famous writer Waco associated with Waco is a transplanted Midwesterner born in Illinois, William Cowper Brann (1855–1898), a satirist whom Mencken called "the past master of invective." Like his contemporary, Ambrose Bierce, author of *The Devil's Dictionary*, Brann brought wit and imagination to his chosen vocation of anatomizing human folly. His ridicule of Baptist hypocrisy gained his journal, *The Iconoclast*, a worldwide circulation of 120,000—a number that is impressive even today—with subscribers throughout the United States and Europe.

In 1895, when a 13-year-old female student from Brazil was raped and impregnated by the son-in-law of Baylor's President, Brann pounced. Mocking the anti-Catholic bigotry of Texan Protestants, Brann declared: "Better a thousand times that she should have wedded a water-carrier in her native land and reared up sturdy sons and daughters of the Church of Rome, than to have been transported to Texas to breed illegitimate Baptists."[5] Fraternity boys from Baylor harassed Brann's wife; repeatedly surrounded his house, making taunts and threats; and eventually kidnapped Brann, beating him until he was almost unconscious while threatening to hang him or shoot him. In the November 1897 issue of *The Iconoclast*, Brann was defiant: "Owing to circumstances entirely beyond my control, I devoted the major part of the past month to digesting a couple of installments of Saving Grace presented by my Baptist brethren, and carefully rubbed in with revolvers and ropes, loaded canes and miscellaneous cudgels."[6]

On April 2, 1898, the day that Brann and his wife were to leave on a tour of San Antonio, Houston, Galveston, and Chicago, a Waco resident named Tom Davis shot Brann in the back and his friend William Ward in the hand as they were walking down the street. Wounded, Brann drew the pistol he carried for protection and shot and killed Davis. Ward recovered, but Brann, shot in the back, the groin, and the foot, soon died. One explanation for the slain killer's motive held "that Davis, who had local political ambitions, would surely corral the Baptist vote (which meant a shoo-in) if he performed a service for them such as exterminating their archenemy."[7] Earlier in February, Brann had written of his newspaper: "There are not Baptists enough in Texas to drive it from this town. If they kill the editor, another and a better man will step into his shoes and continue the old fight against hypocrites and humbugs, against all that loveth and maketh a lie."[8] *The Iconoclast* folded.

Along with its importance to American fundamentalist religion, Waco has long been notorious for racism. From Reconstruction until World War II, Waco was one of the national bases of the Ku Klux Klan (KKK). Klan activity in Waco peaked in 1923, when more than 2,000 members of the KKK held a parade in the city. According to the *Handbook of Texas*, "Many of Waco's business and political leaders at least implicitly supported the Klan during this period, and one member claimed that the Klan 'controlled every office in the city of Waco' during the 1920s."[9] Klansmen and other conservatives in Waco boycotted businesses of residents who did not fall into line. In the 1980s and 1990s, this practice was revived by some factions of the Protestant religious right, who urged their members to patronize only "Christian" businesses—a practice that drew accusations of anti-semitism.

Before the Civil Rights Revolution, George W. Bush's adopted county was thoroughly segregated. In 1955, the Texan historian Frank Goodwyn described the state of race relations during the Eisenhower presidency in the vicinity of Bush's present-day ranch:

> In the cities this condition [economic discrimination] is being fast obliterated, but in the small towns and farm communities, particularly along the Brazos, it persists to this day, protected

largely by the Negroes' ignorance. Education among them is kept at a low ebb, and their activities are limited to the hard labor of the fields. Many of their children pick cotton through the early part of the school year, so that when school opens in September only a few attend. Later, when the cotton season is over, they flood the schoolhouses. In one Brazos bottom Negro school there are two rooms for each grade: a regular room and a "cotton-pickin' room." Until 1954 segregation was practiced generally in the public schools, and the colored schools of many small Texas communities were far inferior to their white schools in facilities and buildings. In the cities, wealthy southerners have poured large quantities of money into Negro school plants in the hope that the fine buildings would dampen the Negro's desire to attend white schools.[10]

The significance of Bush's address during the 2000 Republican primary campaign at Bob Jones University, which banned interracial dating, is therefore apparent. It was not religion alone which made that defiant segregationist university a symbol to the Southern right whose members won Bush the Republican nomination in 2000. Following the court-ordered integration of Waco's public schools, many residents relocated to surrounding suburbs and small towns. Crawford, Texas, which one UPI report described as "a hardscrabble town,"[11] is, among other things, a white-flight suburb of Waco. According to an Austin real estate web site, "many of the town residents are professionals working in Waco who make Crawford their own getaway."[12]

Waco was one of the centers of lynching in the United States. In Texas, 20 percent of the lynchings that claimed 468 victims between 1885 and 1945 took place in a belt of eleven counties along the Brazos River, including McLennan County. (As it happens, the George Herbert Walker Bush Library at Texas A&M in College Station, like the younger Bush's ranch, is in the heart of the historic Texan lynching belt.) Most of the victims of mob violence in Texas as a whole were black (339), although there were also whites (77), Latinos (53), and one Native American. Lynching was all but unknown in the parts of Texas untouched by plantation agriculture; only 15 of 322 incidents occurred outside of East Texas.

The sadism of the white supremacists in Waco and McLennan County has few parallels in the chronicles of human depravity. During Reconstruction, a black ward of U.S. Army Lieutenant A. F. Manning, the local representative of the Freedmen's Bureau assigned to provide for the welfare of freed slaves, was kidnapped and taken to be surgically castrated by two Waco physicians. Federal troops had to be dispatched to prevent white citizens of Waco from freeing one of the doctors after he had been jailed. A few years later, the town was the site of a major race riot, and for decades lynching in the area was common.

Waco achieved international notoriety in 1916. A 17-year-old black youth named Jesse Washington confessed to the crime of murdering Lucy Fyer, the wife of a farmer for whom he had worked. When the judge sentenced him to death by hanging, onlookers seized him and dragged him to the courthouse lawn, where a roaring bonfire had already been built. In front of the courthouse and City Hall, Washington was stripped naked, covered with coal oil, raised up, slowly lowered into the fire—and cooked alive. After he was dead, parts of his charred body were cut off and sold to spectators as souvenirs. Among the cheering crowd were the mayor and police chief of Waco.[13] The "Waco Horror" made headlines throughout the United States and overseas and gave new energy to the anti-lynching movement and the broader campaign for civil rights.

Seventy-seven years later, another horrific fire in the Waco area drew attention from around the world. On April 19, 1993, U.S. government agents using tanks stormed the compound of the Branch Davidians, where David Koresh and his followers had been besieged since they murdered agents of the Bureau of Alcohol, Tobacco, and Firearms during a raid to confiscate illegal firearms in which several of the Davidians were killed. In the fire that broke out in the building—whether by accident or as part of a suicidal plan by Koresh—eighty-one Branch Davidians, including a number of children, were killed. The right wing of the Republican Party denounced the initial raid as well as the disastrous final assault as an example of federal government tyranny, even though Koresh's followers had begun the conflict by gunning down law enforcement officers who were serving warrants. To the right-wing militia movement, some of whose conspiracy theorists describe the federal government as Zionist Occupied

Government (ZOG), Koresh and the Davidians were martyrs in a new American revolution. When Timothy McVeigh blew up the Murrow Federal Building in Oklahoma City, exactly two years later on April 19, 1995, in the most murderous terrorist assault on American soil before the al-Qaeda attacks of September 11, 2001, he did so, he said later, to avenge the death of the Davidians at Waco.

McLennan County, the Texas county that Bush and his publicity staff would like the media and the public to consider a typical example of the wholesome American heartland, is a place that has twice achieved global notoriety: first for the ritual public burning of Jesse Washington and then for the apocalyptic immolation of David Koresh and his cult.

———————————

The LBJ ranch is only an hour's drive from George W. Bush's Prairie Chapel ranch outside of Waco, but it might as well be in another country. Bush's ranch is on the edge of the spongy blackland prairie that stretches to the Gulf of Mexico. Johnson's ranch is found in a rocky landscape that is as different in its traditions as it is distinct in its geography: the Texas Hill Country.

The Texas Hill Country is the traditional name of the Edwards Plateau, the southernmost extension of the Great Plains, the elevated shelf that runs along the eastern edge of the Rocky Mountains from Canada to Central Texas. From the stone ridges of the Edwards Plateau a handful of shallow rivers descend hundreds of feet down the Balcones escarpment and then drain east in parallel stripes across the Gulf Coastal Plains to the sea: the Pedernales, Blanco, Guadalupe, Lampasas, Little, and San Gabriel. One of these, which winds through the Johnson ranch, is the Pedernales River (the name, Anglicized as "Perd'n'Alice," means "peanut" in Spanish). Johnson was born near its banks in 1908, in nearby Stonewall, the son of an impoverished Texas state legislator.

Fourteen miles away from the Johnson ranch is Johnson City, named after one of Lyndon Johnson's relatives. In Johnson City can be found, along the LBJ boyhood home, the Pedernales Electric Cooperative (PEC) headquarters, one of the many rural electric cooperatives that brought light and power to isolated towns and homes in the Hill Country in the 1930s and 1940s. The PEC is a small version of the vast Lower Colorado River Authority (LCRA), a state-chartered utility that operates the chain of dams and artificial lakes along the length of the Colorado River that descend eastward like steps from the hills through Austin. With help from his mentor, President Franklin Roosevelt, Johnson, as a member of Congress in the 1930s, promoted a massive program of dam-building and rural electrification that literally reshaped the landscape of Central Texas.

The Lyndon B. Johnson National Historical Park, comprising more than 1,500 acres, is located next to Blanco County, where Johnson City and Stonewall are found, in Gillespie County. Local traditions are symbolized at the Johnson ranch by pioneer buildings that are German, not Southern. The early settlers of the area were immigrants from Nassau, Hesse, and other parts of western and southwestern Germany, most of whom arrived between the Texas Revolution of 1836 and the Civil War. The German settlers created a society strikingly different from that of the parts of Texas influenced by the American South. In a state renowned for gigantism, the Hill Country has a human scale. Visitors accustomed to hearing Texans boast about the size of their state are often amused when residents of the Hill Country refer to modest hills as "mountains" and bestow the name of "river" on something that elswhere would be considered a creek—or, during the seasons when it is dry, a ravine. The region in which Johnson grew up was a land of small hills, small rivers—and small producers. "Their places can be recognized by their thorough and systematic cultivation," the historian Frank Goodwyn wrote in 1955. "By picking their own cotton and wielding their own hoes, they have grown wealthy."[14] Goodwyn described the cultural gap between the Germans and their southern neighbors: "Beside the Anglo agrarians, there are many communities of German, Czech, and Scandinavian descent whose ancestors were attracted to Texas during her nine years as an independent republic. Having come directly from countries where slavery did not prevail, they show no disposition to depend on servile labor, be it either Negro or Mexican."[15] Writing earlier in 1925, another Texas historian agreed: "Life on the plantation, cultivated by slave labor, was quite different from that on German farms or in German settlements. The planter and slave owner with his family generally indulged in a life of indolence, while on the German farms every member of the family worked continuously, often even on Sundays, using in Texas the same intensive agriculture as formerly in Germany."[16]

There were few helpless poor and few rich people in the Texas Hill Country, which came as close to an egalitarian society as any in the United States. Most people did their own work. Labor was not considered a dishonorable activity to be carried out by helots of a different race or class, as it was in the areas of Texas with plantations, giant ranches, and mines. During a visit to the Hill Country in 1855, Frederick Law Olmsted, who later designed Central Park in Manhattan, was impressed by the contrast between the lethargy and poverty of the Southern-settled areas of Texas and the industriousness of the Texas Germans:

> Half the men now residing in New Braunfels and its vicinity are probably agricultural laborers, or farmers, who themselves follow the plough. The majority of the latter do not, I think, own more than ten acres of land each. Within the town itself, there are of master-mechanics, at least, the following numbers, nearly all of whom employ several workmen: carpenters and builders—20, wagonmakers—7, blacksmiths—8, gun and locksmiths—2, copperers—1, tinsmiths—2, machinists—1, saddlers—3, shoemakers—6, turners—2, tailors—5, button and fringe-makers—1, tanners—3, butchers—3, and bakers—4. . . . There are ten or twelve stores and small tradesmen's shops, two or three apothecaries, and as many physicians, lawyers, and clergymen.[17]

Another writer agreed, contrasting the bourgeois ethic of the Texas Germans with that of the Southerners in Texas: "In the cities [of Texas], trades and industries were in the hands of German mechanics and tradesmen, while the Americans were generally restricted to the vocations of lawyer, physician, civil engineer, banker, broker, land agent, lumberman, etc."[18]

Just as they did not despise labor, the German Texans did not despise leisure or learning. Their beer-gardens rang with the melodies of their singing clubs, and scholarship, journalism, and the composition of verse in German and English were valued in a society founded by surplus nobles and refugee professors from Central Europe. The obsession of the Southern evangelical Protestants to the east and north with sins like dancing, drinking, and card-playing was alien to Lutherans, Catholics, and free-thinkers alike. The Germans voted against candidates who supported Prohibition, in an era in which the Baptists and other evangelicals wanted to outlaw liquor.

The informal capital of the German Hill Country is Fredericksburg, today a tourist destination popular with weekend visitors from Austin, San Antonio, and other Texan cities. Fredericksburg is only an hour's drive from Waco, but the cultural distance between them is as vast as that between Lincoln, Nebraska, and Birmingham, Alabama. As you drive from the Johnson ranch through Fredericksburg, you notice the names of the cross streets: Washington, Lincoln, Adams. These are the names of presidents in the Federalist-Whig-Republican tradition—the historic rival of the Jeffersonian-Jacksonian tradition that produced the Confederates, the segregationist Southern Democrats, and today's Southern conservative Republicans. Johnson grew up a few miles from a town whose very street names advertised the contempt of its inhabitants for the Southern Democrats and the Confederate Lost Cause. In the early twentieth century, many German Texans supported the progressive Republicans Theodore Roosevelt and Robert La Follette. Even when the Democrat Lyndon Johnson was their most famous neighbor, during a time when the rest of Texas was solidly Democratic, many of the Hill Country Germans voted Republican—because the Republican Party was the party of Lincoln and the Democrats were the party of slavery and secession.

Not far from Fredericksburg is the small town of Comfort. Here is found a monument listing German-Texan names, and one Mexican-Texan name, with the inscription *"Treue der Union"*—True to the Union. In the middle of a former Confederate state, this is a monument to soldiers who died for the cause of the Union in the Civil War—a group of about sixty Texas German volunteers, along with a handful of Anglo-Texan and Mexican-Texan Unionists, who were massacred in 1862 by Confederate troops near the Nueces River southwest of the Hill Country.

In addition to being a center of Unionism and anti-slavery sentiment, Comfort was a center of "free-thinking," or secularism. The local tradition of secular funerals persisted into the twentieth century. Many of the small towns in the area of the Johnson ranch bear traces of the secularism and radicalism of expatriate German intellectuals in the 1840s and 1850s. Boerne—now practically a suburb of San Antonio—is named after Ludwig Boerne, a radical Jewish journalist in early-nineteenth-century Germany. The nearby town of Bettina commemorates Bettina von Arnim, a pioneer German feminist. Then there were the "Lateiner" settlements—so-called because the German settlers were educated academics and professionals who would hold debates and symposia in Latin in their frontier cabins. One farm was originally named Tusculum, after one of the rural villas of the Roman republican statesman, philosopher, and orator Cicero—a hero to German liberals and radicals who rejected monarchy for republicanism. Writes one historian:

> The "Latin settlement" had been born—a library of the ancient and modern classics was to be found in almost every house and the latest products of literature were eagerly read and discussed at the weekly meetings of these gentleman farmers at the school house. It sometimes occurred at these meetings that Comanches stood listening at the open door, while one of the Latin farmers was lecturing on the socialistic theories of St. Simon or Fourier.[19]

The symbol of the philosophical and religious pluralism of the Hill Country is the *Vereinskirche*, or "Society Church," a striking octagonal building in the central square in Fredericksburg (the present structure is a replica of the original, built in the 1930s). During the early years of the German colony, the *Vereinskirche* was used as a church or meeting place by Catholics, Lutherans, and free-thinkers who respected one another's rights, if not one another's beliefs.

The founding father and patron saint of the German Hill Country was an intellectual himself. Ottfried Hans Freiherr von Meusebach was a German aristocrat who in 1845 renounced his inherited title and became John O. Meusebach, commisioner-general of the Society for the Protection of German Immigrants in Texas. Meusebach's father was an enlightened nobleman and amateur literary scholar fond of repeating the maxim, *Gedanken sind Zoll frei*, "Thoughts are toll-free." The Meusebachs were friends of Jacob and Wilhelm Grimm, fellow liberals and the authors of the famous collection of German fairy tales, and of Bettina von Arnim, a feminist intellectual whose youthful correspondence with Goethe, Germany's greatest writer, was published by the elder Meusebach in 1835 under the title *Goethe's Correspondence with a Child*. Disgusted by the political repression in Germany, then divided among Prussia, Austria, and petty principalities, John O. Meusebach hoped to found *der freie Verein*, the free society, in Texas. For decades he was the principal leader of the Hill Country Germans whose informal center was Fredericksburg, where Baron's Creek is named after him. The settlers endured bankruptcies, epidemics, Indian raids, and murders and assaults carried out by Confederate troops and Southern outlaws and vigilante mobs during and after the Civil War.

In his retirement, Meusebach lived in a cottage in a place he named Loyal Valley in honor of the Union cause in the Civil War. In a state associated with slave plantations and vast cattle ranches, the democratic baron literally cultivated his garden, described by a visitor in 1877: "Loyal Valley is indeed a garden in a wilderness; a garden in which one can linger and be happy. Here is a nursery in which sixty varieties of roses grow, and hundreds of the finest flora of three continents; sixty varieties of pear, forty of peach, and an array of apples, plums, and grapes—all cultivated and arranged with taste and skill that cannot be excelled. It is curious to see such an industry in so isolated and remote a region."[20] Meusebach's horticultural interests were shared by his neighbors. The German Hill Country became famous for its peach orchards—as small and intensely cultivated by their owners as Texan plantations and ranches have often been huge and carelessly worked by gangs of poor blacks, whites, or Latinos on behalf of absentee landlords.

Meusebach, an amateur scientist, had an ample library, according to his grand-daughter: "He received the *Congressional Record* regularly. His library, though not as complete as his father's in Berlin, was rich in books. Darwin, with his bold pronouncements, appealed to Meusebach and books on travel and maps surrounded him. Goethe's volumes were always within reach, with certain pages worn from reading."[21] Bibliophilia was a trait of the leaders of the German and Scandinavian settlements in Central Texas. Sir Svante Palm, the Swedish nobleman who helped settle poor Swedes in Central Texas and opposed the secession of Texas along with the loyal Unionist Sam Houston during the Civil War, had a library of 12,000 volumes that he bequeathed to the University of Texas at Austin.

The moment of greatest peril in Meusebach's life may have come during his negotiations with the Comanche Indians, whose hunting grounds the German settlers had entered. The Comanches were newcomers in the Hill Country themselves, having displaced the Apaches, who in turn had migrated into the area in the seventeenth and eighteenth centuries from the northern Plains. While many Southerners in Texas brought with them from the South a genocidal hatred of all Native Americans, the German settlers were liberals and radicals with idealistic notions about human brotherhood.

On March 1, 1847, near the San Saba River, several dozen German, Anglo, and Mexican-Texans met with several hundred Comanche warriors under the leadership of three chiefs: Mopechucope, Santa Anna, and Buffalo Hump. Meusebach and his aides rode slowly up and down in front of the warriors—and then, to everyone's surprise, they calmly and deliberately emptied their guns into the air, demonstrating to the Comanches that they were now unarmed. This dramatic demonstration of confidence in the peaceable intentions of the Comanches worked. The two sides negotiated a treaty which, although violated by some on both sides, was an overall success. Colonel Jack Hays, the most famous Texas Ranger of all time, informed Meusebach that "he was never molested [by Indians] nor lost any animals during his travel within the limits of our colony, but as soon as he had passed the line he had losses."[22] In his speech to the Comanches, Meusebach shared a vision of racial harmony and intermarriage unthinkable to white Southerners of the era: "When my people have lived with you for some time, and when we know each other better, then it may happen that some wish to marry. . . . I do not disdain my red brethren because their skin is darker, and I do not think more of the white people because their complexion is lighter."[23] The Comanches, impressed by Meusebach's red hair and beard, nicknamed him El Sol Colorado—The Red Sun.

Every year on March 6 visitors from other parts of Texas and the United States, arriving in San Antonio, an hour south of Fredericksburg, witness a ceremony commemorating the battle of the Alamo that took place in 1836. All but unknown, outside of the nearby Hill Country, is the annual Easter Fires celebration, which commemorates, not a battle, but conflict averted by the peace treaty between Meusebach and the Comanches. Each year, in view of that symbol of religious and philosophical pluralism, the *Vereinskirche*, Native Americans join the festivities; traditional German folk music mingles with the drums of a powwow in a celebration of interracial peace.*

Racial and ethnic pluralism was as characteristic of the Hill Country as a hierarchical white/black caste system was of East Texas and the Deep South and an Anglo/Latino caste system was of South Texas. In addition to the Germans, some Southerners left their mark on the historic culture of the Hill Country. In the nineteenth century, tall "cedar" trees—not cedar at all, but mountain juniper, a conifer related to pine—were harvested to make furniture or firewood or charcoal. (Today's cedar woods are clusters of new-growth bushes, pathetic remnants of the once-tall cedar forests.) Much of the work was done

-----

*The building of bonfires on hilltops at Easter was a custom in the parts of Germany from which many of the settlers came. The custom in Texas, however, is explained by reference to the negotiations between Meusebach and the Comanches. While the men of Fredericksburg were away, to either make peace or fight the Comanches, some children were frightened by the Comanche watch fires in the distance. A German mother reassured them by telling them that the Easter bunny (another German export to the United States) was boiling eggs to be painted for Easter.

by poor Southern whites from the Ozarks and Appalachia known to the local residents as "cedar-choppers." Like their relatives in the Highland South from West Virginia through Tennesseee to Texas, these "hillbillies" were often squatters on land they did not legally own. They fluctuated between being a white rural proletariat and a white rural underclass, accounting for much of the crime and poverty in the area. During the era of Prohibition between World War I and the 1930s, some of them became "moonshiners," making contraband alcohol in stills located in inaccessible, wooded valleys and mountainsides, where whole families would live in squalid conditions in tiny shacks or stone cabins.

Like their equivalents in the Ozark-Appalachian mountain chain, the Hill Country cedar-choppers tended to be apolitical and suspicious of authority. To the extent that they influenced politics, it was in the direction of populism and radicalism. For generations, many poor whites of the Southern hills had been hostile to the rich white planters who monopolized the good farmlands along the river bottoms and coasts—lands often appropriated from squatters who lacked title or were cheated because they had no political connections or legal knowledge. (Abraham Lincoln's father, who lost his land in Kentucky and moved to Indiana and then Illinois for this reason, was one.) During the Civil War, support for the Union was strongest in parts of the back-country South; East Tennessee supplied soldiers for the Federal Army, while West Virginia seceded from planter-controlled Confederate Virginia and joined the Union cause. In the mixture of influences that created the relatively progressive culture of the Texas Hill Country, then, the populist instincts of poor back-country Southern whites must be added to the anti-slavery tradition and liberal nationalism of the more educated and affluent German pioneers.

Yet another influence was the presence of a small group of black residents in the Hill Country with a significant history. Johnson, who did more to help black Americans than any president since Lincoln, grew up not far from what was locally known as "the colony," made up of descendants of freed slaves who moved to the Hill Country during Reconstruction. Peyton Colony in Blanco County, the county in which Johnson was born, was founded around 1865 by Peyton

Roberts, a former slave from Lockhart, Texas. During Reconstruction, Roberts and other freedmen from Texas and other Southern states acquired land in eastern Blanco County. The center of the colony was Mount Horeb Baptist Church; there was also a schoolhouse, a post office, and a boarding house. Surrounded by German families, the black families were safer than they would have been elsewhere. Some of these black Hill Country Texans even learned German from their neighbors and employers. Descendants of the original settlers live in the region to this day.

The two major cities nearest to the Johnson ranch are San Antonio and Austin. Austin, the state capital, includes the Balcones divide within its city limits, so that it has always had a schizophrenic character—its flat, low eastern part belongs to the Deep South, while its hilly, rocky west is the perimeter of the Great Plains. Cotton was grown along the banks of the Colorado River, which runs through Austin, and the fields next to it, and from the 1840s on Austin had a large population of whites and blacks from the South. However, there was also a significant German element, which may explain why Austin and Travis County voted against secession along with the German counties to the west in 1860.

The two landmarks that define the Austin skyline are the pink-granite dome of the state capitol building and the ashen limestone tower of the University of Texas a few blocks to the north. For generations, the capitol dome and the tower have been at war. Populist politicians with their base in East Texas have denounced the university as a center of secular humanism and socialism. In the early twentieth century, one governor, James Ferguson, better known as "Pa" Ferguson or "Farmer Jim," accused professors at the University of Texas of trying to grow hair on the backs of armadillos (a project that has yet to attract the attention of today's thriving biotech industry in Texas). Another governor, W. Lee "Pass the Biscuits, Pappy" O'Daniel, supported the conservative university regents when, on November 1, 1944, they fired the university's president, Homer Rainey, for, among other things, allowing students to read the novel *USA* by John Dos

Passos and for tolerating professors with liberal views on race and economics. University students marched the few blocks from the campus to the state capitol, imitating mourners; a coffin bore the legend, ACADEMIC FREEDOM IS DEAD.* In the 1970s, Austin became the capital of the "outlaw country music" of Willie Nelson and Waylon Jennings; in the 1990s, the film and TV producers Richard Linklater and Mike Judge turned it into a dynamic center of new media, and Austin's annual "South by Southwest" festival became one of the most famous film and music festivals in the world. The growth of the Austin computer industry as a result of the exertions of natives like Michael Dell of Dell computers and immigrants from elsewhere in the United States and the world has given the rocky chalk hills of the Edwards Plateau to the west of Austin where many high-tech research parks are now found a new name: the Silicon Hills.

The other major city near the Johnson ranch is San Antonio, the site of the battle of the Alamo and home to continuous habitation by Mexican and Mexican-American families since the eighteenth century. Between the Civil War and the early twentieth century, the population was one of the most pluralist in the state, mingling Mexican-, German-, and Anglo-Texans. Home to progressive German Republicans in the nineteenth century, San Antonio was known for its left-wing New Deal Democrats in the 1930s.

Indeed, the term "maverick" has its origins in San Antonio. One of San Antonio's prominent nineteenth-century citizens, a veteran of the Texas Revolution named Samuel Maverick, was in the habit of letting his cattle roam unbranded; the term "maverick," used by his neighbors for an unbranded calf, came to mean first a deviant politician and then an independent individual. His grandson, Maury Maverick, a left-wing New Deal Democrat, who was mayor of San Antonio in the 1930s and later the only Southern member of Congress who

---

*UT students retain their cherished tradition of irreverence. When I was an undergraduate at UT-Austin in the early 1980s, the student body, weary of the monopolization of student offices by wealthy fraternity boys and sorority girls from Houston and Dallas, elected as president of the student body a cartoon character—Hank the Hallucination.

voted for federal anti-lynching legislation, contributed another neologism to the English language. In the *New York Times Magazine* of May 21, 1944, Maverick—then chairman of the U.S. Smaller War Plants Committee in the House of Representatives—coined the term "gobbledegook" for obscure bureaucratic jargon. He said later that bureaucratic language reminded him of a Texas turkey, "always gobbledy gobbling and strutting with ludicrous pomposity. At the end of this gobble there was a sort of gook." His revolutionary temperament is apparent in one of his proposals: "Anyone using the words 'activation' or 'implementation' will be shot."

While the Waco/Crawford area is infamous for its violent religious fanatics and its shocking lynchings, the Hill Country has long been a haven for mavericks of all kinds—the very sort of people who are not welcome among many of George W. Bush's neighbors. The capital of Hill Country eccentricity is a few miles from the Johnson ranch in the same county, Gillespie County. Founded by Jacob Luckenbach, a German immigrant and a veteran of the Texas Revolution, Luckenbach has given not one but two famous mavericks to the world—a remarkable achievement for a town whose official population in the late twentieth century was three.

Four decades before Orville and Wilbur Wright flew at Kitty Hawk, on September 20, 1865, an immigrant schoolteacher and inventor from Wurtemburg named Jacob Friedrich Brodbeck (1821–1910), is said to have flown his own experimental airplane around a hundred feet before it disintegrated, leaving him unharmed in a field three miles east of Luckenbach. In 1971, the "town"—a few acres—was sold by one Benno Engel to a resident of nearby Comfort named John Russell "Hondo" Crouch. Inspired, perhaps, by the free-thinking tradition of Comfort, or remembering the importance in local Hill Country history of the titled promoters of German colonization in Texas, Prince Solms von Braunfels and Baron von Meusebach, Hondo Crouch (as he was called) proclaimed himself mayor and clown prince of Luckenbach and declared that Luckenbach was "a free state . . . of mind." In the years that followed, Hondo Crouch and his two fellow citizens became icons of the counterculture, as they presided over festivals like the Luckenbach Great World's Fair and an annual Hug-In. (Needless to say, Hug-Ins of the kind found along Ranch Road 1376 in the Hill Country are frowned upon in the vicinity of Prairie Chapel Road, the address of the Bush ranch in Crawford, Texas.) Hondo Crouch, who died in 1976, was immortalized by Waylon Jennings's hit 1977 song "Luckenbach, Texas (Back to the Basics of Love)." In 1995, Luckenbach was the site of one of Austin resident Willie Nelson's annual Fourth of July picnics—a kind of Texan Woodstock festival.

Most German Texans have always tended to be conservative in their mores and strict in their manners, and many of them were—and are—devout Lutherans and Catholics. Why, then, did the Hill Country become a haven over the generations to an assortment of freed slaves, eccentric inventors, early free-thinkers, anarchic hillbillies, and college-town hippies? The answer is simple: *even if they disliked strangers and nonconformists, conservative German Texans would not attack them.* In the regions of Texas infused with traditional Southern culture, by contrast, deviance in political views, religious belief, behavior, or even dress could—and sometimes still can—subject one to ostracism, verbal harassment, physical beatings, or even murder. A small-*m* maverick in the vicinity of the present-day Johnson ranch could always be certain that his life and property would be secure. Throughout most of the history of Texas, a maverick living near the present-day Bush ranch could not be sure about his safety. Remember the fate of William Cowper Brann.

––––––––––––––––

The core of Johnson country can be thought of as a triangle whose corners are three monumental structures: the octagonal tower of the non-sectarian *Vereinskirche* in Fredericksburg; the small spire of the monument to the martyrs of the Union in Comfort; and the pale tower of the University of Texas, an island of intellect in a sea of Southern anti-intellectualism and Protestant fundamentalism. Within and around this imaginary triangle is a rocky Great Plains landscape, divided into small, productive family farms in the nineteenth century and transformed in the twentieth by artificial lakes behind steep dams that hum with the power sent rippling through electrical towers above the oak and cedar hills. This is a region of Texas where the names of small towns—Boerne, Bettina—evoke nineteenth-century German crusaders for women's rights and liberal democracy, a region of Texas where streets like Adams and Washington and Lincoln are named after the heroes of the American liberal nationalist tradition, strongest in New England and the Midwest, which has opposed the Confederates and the Southern segregationists, a region of Texas where the best-known local legend commemorates not a battle but a peace treaty between European settlers and Native Americans.

Lyndon Johnson's roots in Texas went far deeper than those of the Bush family. But his roots were in a Texas very different from theirs. George H. W. Bush moved to, and George W. Bush grew up in, a West Texas that was homogeneous in race, ethnicity, and religion—a land of Anglo-Celtic Southern Protestants for whom the three major world religions were the Baptists, the Methodists, and the Church of Christ. Lyndon Johnson, by contrast, grew up in a pluralistic society of German Lutherans and German Catholics, Southern evangelical Protestants, Mexican-Americans, and black Americans, in which the Southern Protestants were a minority in much of the area. Bush's neighbors in West Texas, like his later neighbors in the suburbs of Waco, included a few wealthy immigrants from the Northeast like his father, but were predominantly Southerners whose ancestors had supported the Confederacy and often the Ku Klux Klan. Johnson, although he was predominantly of Southern descent, matured in a community that had been the center of Unionism in Texas during the Civil War—a section of a one-party Democratic state where many people voted Republican out of loyalty to the party of Lincoln and despised Jefferson Davis and Robert E. Lee. Bush spent his boyhood in a part of Texas in which many right-wing segregationist Democrats preferred Goldwater to Johnson in 1964. Johnson's Texas was one shaped by two local traditions of opposition to the conservative Democrats who dominated Texas politics—the traditions of the liberal and socialist German Unionists and the radical white Southern Populists.

Bush's West Texas, like his adopted Crawford in East Texas, had much in common in culture with the Deep South. Bush emerged from the same Southern tradition that produced Strom Thurmond and George Wallace and that gave Barry Goldwater and Ronald Reagan and his own father its support. Johnson was described as the first Southern president since the Civil War, but this was not really true. While Texas as a whole was a Southern state, Johnson came from the anomalous piece of the Midwest embedded in its core. To achieve national prominence, he sometimes had to disguise his principles in order not to offend the state's Southern majority. But his native region, in its liberal and nationalist political culture and its German and Scandinavian influences, resembled progressive prairie states like Wisconsin, Nebraska, and Minnesota, which produced his vice-president and fellow champion of racial equality, Hubert Humphrey.

Cultural geography is of little use in analyzing the personalities of politicians—but it is indispensable in understanding their politics. Political leaders are shaped by many influences, and the more important politicians, as they grow in stature, must appeal to more diverse constituencies and may alter their policies and their views. Even so, successful politicians reflect the values of their neighbors and constituents; if they did not, they would never have risen to high office. The fact that George W. Bush is a product of the Deep South tradition of the cotton plantation country, transplanted to the West Texas oil region, while Lyndon Johnson grew up in a region shaped by German-American Unionism, liberalism, and anti-slavery sentiment, does much to explain the remarkable differences between these radically different presidents from Texas. Where you are on the political spectrum depends a lot on where you are from.

TWO

The Confederate Century

In Russia, where overt dissent has been banned through most of its history, a tradition of silent satire takes the form of the sale of hollow ceramic dolls, nested inside one another. The removal of the top half of Gorbachev's body might reveal Stalin, hidden within. A Russian doll that contrasts the image with the reality of Texas might be a statuette of a Western cowboy, which, when dismantled, would reveal a white-suited Southern planter. Texas is a Southern state masquerading as a Western state.

The second largest state of the United States in population, Texas is the second largest in area, after Alaska. Bigger than Germany, Texas could contain within its territory all of the New England states, New York, New Jersey, Pennsylvania, Delaware, Maryland, Ohio, Kentucky, and the District of Columbia.[1] Within the borders of Texas three regions of the North American continent meet: the South, the Plains, and the Southwest. The Central Texan Hill Country and the Staked Plains and Panhandle to the north represent the southernmost extension of the Great Plains, which stretch north to Canada and include eastern Colorado, Oklahoma, Kansas, Nebraska, Wyoming, and the Dakotas. The Southwest extends into West Texas and South Texas (known in Texas as "the Valley," after the Rio Grande Valley). The Plains and the Southwest have supplied the mingled imagery of Texas—cowboys and Indians from the Plains, Latino imagery from the Southwest.

But the parts of Texas that are in the Plains and the Southwest are not the heart of Texas, even though they account for about three-quarters of the state's area and define its popular image as a Western state. The core of Texas, the dominant region, is and always has been East Texas—the green, well-watered, humid, wooded, and flat area to the east of Austin and the north of Houston and Galveston. Here, from the days of the Republic of Texas in the 1840s until the present, most of the Texan population has been concentrated—along with most political power and wealth.

East Texas is the westernmost extension of the Deep South. For generations, its economy was based on cotton, picked by a black labor force that was first enslaved and then segregated. The society of East Texas, like that of the Deep South states, was biracial and hierarchical. East Texas had nothing in common with Plains states like Nebraska or Southwestern states like New Mexico or Arizona. It was a clone of the society of Alabama, Mississippi, Georgia, and northern Florida (but not Louisiana, with its unique Cajun element).

Texas was a pluralist society in its origins, and it has become pluralist again as the result of immigration from other parts of the United States, a process that started during World War II, as well as immigration from other parts of the world following the liberalization of America's restrictive immigration laws in the 1960s. But Texas was not merely part of the South, but part of the Deep South, during the Confederate Century between 1876 and the 1970s. The Confederates in Texas and similar Southern states lost the Civil War, but by means of terrorist violence they drove out Federal troops and defeated Reconstruction. In the territory of the former Confederacy they created a de facto Confederacy, with the economy of a non-industrial resource colony, the social order of a racial caste society, and the politics of a one-party dictatorship. The Confederate order in Texas was undermined by the New Deal, but it took the Civil Rights Revolution to shatter it. And the Confederate tradition continues to influence politics in Texas and, through Texan conservatives in Washington like President George W. Bush, the nation and the world.

———

Texas has had four major "tribes": Anglo-Celtic Southerners, Tejanos (Mexican-Texans), Germans, and blacks. (Native American nations like the Cherokees, Comanches, and Apaches were small and quickly defeated and deported.) To summarize the history of Texas from 1836 until the 1960s in one sentence: the biggest tribe, the Anglo-Celtic Southerners, expropriated the Tejanos, deported the Indians, crushed the Germans, and exploited the blacks.

The secession of Texas from Mexico in 1835–1836 was supported by a diverse coalition of Anglo-Celtic Southerners, Tejanos, and Germans. During the ten-year existence of Texas as an independent republic, before its annexation by the United States in 1846, there was a flood of Southerners, many of them slaveowners. Many Tejanos were cheated out of their land, and some emigrated to Mexico. Those who remained were concentrated in South Texas, where they suffered discrimination at the hands of the white Protestants in the towns (many of them Midwestern immigrants) and worked for great Anglo-Texan landowners, who doubled as political bosses and controlled the Mexican-Texan vote. Until immigration from Mexico and other parts of Latin America expanded the Latino population of the state in the last quarter of the twentieth century, Tejanos had little political power.

"The population element of ranking importance in the development of early social cleavages in Texas was the Germans," a Texas historian wrote in 1925.[2] The largest group of non-Southern whites in early Texas were immigrants from Germany—many of them liberals and socialists who had fled Central Europe after the failure of the Revolutions of 1848. While Germans settled throughout the state, the largest concentration was in the Texas Hill Country west of Austin and north of San Antonio (discussed in the previous chapter). Like German immigrants in the North, who provided Lincoln and the Republicans with many voters and leaders, the Texas Germans for the most part opposed slavery, found Southern culture abhorrent, and voted against the secession ordinance in 1860. Following the Civil War, former German Unionists took part in the Reconstruction regime in Texas, where some of them united with black politicians to lobby for the division of Texas into several states, to prevent the ex-Confederate Democrats from taking power once again. Had the divisionists succeeded, one or more states formed from West Texas—Lincoln was one suggested name— would have joined the progressive prairie states like Kansas and

Nebraska, and the South would have ended in the vicinity of Austin. But the divisionist movement failed, and the German Texans lost power along with their white Southern Unionist and black allies when the federal government abandoned Reconstruction in 1876. Adolph Douai, a liberal San Antonio newspaper editor, left Texas after the Civil War, moved to the Northeast, and introduced the German institution of the kindergarten to the United States. The traumatized German-Texan community was harassed again during World War I. While much of the Hill Country retains a German character to this day, the dynamic culture of its liberal and intellectual founding fathers withered during generations of Southern persecution.

Black Texans were even more brutally subjugated by the dominant Anglo-Celtic ethnic group. During Reconstruction, Texan schools were integrated and blacks were elected to the legislature, but after Federal troops were withdrawn in 1876, conservative Democrats "redeemed" Texas and the other states. The Texas constitution of 1876 eliminated most of the progressive reforms enacted during Reconstruction and established a minimal government that reflected Confederate/Jeffersonian ideals. In the next two decades, during which the Democratic Party and the Ku Klux Klan were largely interchangeable, Democrats used violence to prevent black Texans from voting or holding office. The violence was at its most intense in East Texas, where blacks outnumbered whites in some counties:

> Such violence was aided and abetted by men in high places such as Judge O.D. Cannon, who was district judge [of Robertson County in East Texas] from 1890 to 1900. He killed one black legislator (Hal Geiger), and wounded another (Alexander Asberry). Cannon was not very discriminatory in meting out violence, for he also killed three white men. In 1896, Cannon, as well as other Democrats, decided to put an end to black rule. When the election of state and county officers took place in November, forty men armed with Winchesters positioned themselves at the polling place in Franklin, Texas, to turn away blacks who came to vote. In order to make sure that blacks would not brave past these forty men, O.D. Cannon stood at the door of the election booth with his six-shooter in his hand. At another precinct, blacks were marched four abreast out of the polling

place and told not to stop. In order to enforce this edict, two of Cannon's deputies stood at the election room door, one with a gun and the other with a baseball bat. This election not only wrote the end to "black rule" in Robertson County, but also signaled the end of the election of blacks to the state legislature in the post-Reconstruction era.[3]

In 1893, a report of the Republican minority in the U.S. House of Representatives concluded that "through Kuklux violence in nearly all the Southern communities the Democratic party gradually gained control of every branch of the State governments. The murders and assassinations committed have passed into history. . . . Although there are still occasional instances of violence, this is no longer necessary because the laws are so framed that the Democrats can keep themselves in possession of the governments in every Southern State."[4]

In other parts of the United States, local ethnic and religious majorities managed to share power and opportunity with minority groups, even if there were tensions. Why was the Anglo-Celtic Southern Protestant tribe in Texas so intolerant even of other white ethnic groups like the immigrant Germans?

The answer is found in their history. By the time they reached Texas, the Anglo-Celtic ancestors of most of today's white Texans had been conquering and expropriating other ethnic nations for centuries. Originally they were Protestant Scots whom the English planted in conquered Ulster on land stolen from the native Catholic Irish. Having displaced the native Irish in Ulster, some Scots-Irish families crossed the Atlantic to the Ozarks and Appalachians, where (with a few exceptions, like Sam Houston and Davy Crockett) they supported the ethnic cleansing of the civilized, literate Cherokee Indians. They brought with them to the American South one of their denominations, the "ironside Baptists"—a term that originated in the seventeenth century among British Protestants fighting in the army of Oliver Cromwell.

The swaggering Texan is nothing more than the Scots-Irish frontiersman—a more recent version of the stereotypical "Kaintuck" portrayed in early-nineteenth-century American literature and popular drama, before the Texan cowboy became a cliché. The career in fact and legend of David Crockett, the Tennessean frontier politician who died defending the Alamo during the Texas Revolution, symbolizes the westward movement of this Scots-Irish archetype. The imagery of the Texan cowboy may be that of northern Mexico (the cowboy or vaquero costume, the lariat and horse, the ranch), but the spirit is that of the mountaineers of the Appalachians and Ozarks.

Centuries spent conquering frontier lands—first from the Irish, then from the American Indians and Mexicans—and exploiting the labor of others (the Catholic Irish in northern Ireland, blacks, Mexican-Americans, and not least other Southern whites) turned the Anglo-Celtic Southerners who have dominated Texas into a people as militaristic as the ancient Spartans. Southerners have always been over-represented among American soldiers—and among American perpetrators of homicide and among devoted supporters of capital punishment like George W. Bush. The legendary feuding families, the Hatfields and McCoys, were, of course, Scots-Irish.

Texan violence is neither a "Western" phenomenon nor a "frontier" phenomenon. The homicide rates in parts of the Mountain West and Great Plains and prairie settled by New Englanders and Germans and Scandinavians are very low, although these regions were part of the western frontier more recently than most of Texas. The Germans and Scandinavians and Anglo-American Midwesterners on the Texas frontier did not shoot one another in great numbers. Texan violence is part of the cultural legacy of the Old South rather than of the Old West. Hollywood to the contrary, the South, not the West, is and always has been the most violent section of the United States. This, too, was part of the cultural heritage of the Anglo-Celtic Protestants who migrated from the northern British border to Ulster, the Southern hills, and then Texas.

The Anglo-Celtic tradition produced what D. W. Meining described as the "Typical Texan" in 1969 in terms that remain relevant today:

> The Texan emerges from these investigations as one who is strongly individualistic and egalitarian, optimistic and utilitarian, volatile and chauvinistic, ethnocentric and provincial, as one still

very much under the influence of older rural and moral traditions. Such a person regards government as no more than a necessary evil, and accepts violence as an appropriate solution to
certain kinds of personal and group problems. Material wealth is
much admired for its own sake but industriousness has no particular virtue; land has prestige, but especially in the form of the
ranch or the plantation, for cattle and cotton have symbolic value
while manual field work should be left to Negroes. Thus the security of the small family farm ranks very low on the scale of values. There is an easy acceptance of equality among one's own
kind but a rigid sense of superiority over other local peoples, and
a deep suspicion of outsiders as threats to the social order. The
narrow moral strictures of Protestant fundamentalism are
accepted as an ideal moral code but certain covert violations are
routinely tolerated (such as the use of hard liquor).[5]

The other Southern type—the "cavalier" or aristocratic colonel of
the plantation house civilization in the coastal South—has not contributed to the popular image of Texas. Even so, the Texan franchise
of the propertied Southern upper class traditionally has run the state,
not the Scots-Irish "hillbillies," "crackers," or "rednecks." In Texas,
where the streams of westward migration from the South ended, the
cultures of the hill South and the coastal plantation South have been
blurred and mixed to a greater degree than in other Southern states.

It is often said that Texas, having been a sovereign republic from
1836 to 1845, has always retained a distinct sense of its own independence. Nothing could have been further from the truth during the
Confederate Century, when Texas was a loyal member of the Solid
South. Texas may have called itself "the Lone Star State," but in
national politics it acted in unison with Alabama, Mississippi, Georgia, and the other Deep South states. If there was a nation-within-a-
nation, it was not Texas, but the Confederacy.

As a symbol of Texas, the free-spirited cowboy was far from apt.
Individuals willing to stand up to public opinion might be found in
New England or on the West Coast, but not in the Southern-settled
parts of Texas. The Anglo-Celtic Southerner, in Texas as elsewhere, was
a not a freedom-loving individualist but a freedom-fearing conformist,

who combined physical bravery with intellectual and political cow-
ardice. Outside of the anomalous Hill Country/Central Texas region,
where ethnic diversity created a pocket of cultural and intellectual
pluralism, toleration of deviance in politics, religion, morals, and even
dress was all but non-existent, and non-conformists could expect
ostracism if not violent assault. Instead of the lone cowboy, the character that best symbolized the dominant Texan culture during the
Confederate Century was a plural figure: the lynch mob.

Official Texan patriotism, during the Confederate Century, was as
much of a fraud as the cowboy myth. The Texan patriotism cultivated
by the Southern oligarchs of Texas was neither genuinely Texan nor
genuinely patriotic. It was not genuinely Texan because its definition
of the Texan people left out not only black and Latino Texans, but also
the substantial minority of white Texans who were not ethnic white
Southerners or who had Southern Unionist antecedents. It was not
genuinely patriotic because it put the interests of the "South"—
defined not only as the white South but as the rich families of the
white South—above the interests of the state of Texas and the United
States. Regions like the South have no place in our constitutional system; and yet the Southern Texans, during the Civil War and Reconstruction and the Confederate Century, consistently subordinated the
interests of Texas to those of the Solid South, while counseling trai-
torous resistance to federal authority whenever it threatened the
Southern social order.

During the Confederate Century, then, the Lone Star State was
anything but independent in its relations with the rest of the country.
If South and West and North Texas were colonies of East Texas, East
Texas itself was a colony of the Deep South, and its oligarchs took
their inspiration from the landlords of the black-belt counties in states
like Alabama, Mississippi, and Georgia. Whether the subject was
secession, redemption, literacy tests and poll taxes, or massive resistance to federal court desegregation orders, the influence ran from
east to west, from the Deep South to East Texas and, through the state
legislature in Austin, to all of Texas. When Lyndon Johnson, then Senate majority leader, refused to sign the segregationist "Southern Manifesto" in 1956, this was considered treason by those Texans who were

loyal white Southerners before they were loyal Texans. The neo-Confederate Texans could not even be creative in their wickedness; theirs was an imported and derivative evil. How proud could intelligent and humane Texans be of a state that copied its civil rights legislation in 1902 from that advanced society, that vanguard of human progress and enlightenment, the state of Mississippi?

The saying that "The winners write the history" is not always true; in Texas and the other states of the former Confederacy, the losers wrote the history (assuming, that is, that the Confederates lost; if maintaining white supremacy and their social and political primacy was more important to them than formal independence, then the Southern planters won the Civil War). Until the 1990s, when they were discreetly removed, the grounds of the state capitol in Austin were a forest of statues of Confederate soldiers. Until the 1970s, Robert E. Lee's birthday was a state holiday, along with Washington's and Lincoln's. In books written by and for Anglo-Celtic Texans, Reconstruction was a terrible time, in which a coalition of white immigrant carpetbaggers from the North and local, lower-class white scalawags teamed up with freed slaves to brutalize "the people" of Texas, until Northern tyranny ended in 1876. Anglo-Celtic Texans, like other white Southerners, took pride in their Confederate ancestors. In conversation they would assure one that the Civil War was about states' rights and had nothing to do with slavery. In the official version of Texas history, no Mexicans appeared after the battle of San Jacinto, and there were no black Texans and no German Texans and no white Southern Unionists (unless one counts those mysterious traitors to the South, the scalawags, who appeared out of nowhere in 1865 and vanished just as mysteriously in 1876). Unwilling to share power with the other ethnic groups in Texas, the Anglo-Celtic Southern tribe was also unwilling to share history. The other Texans were not demonized by the tribal historians; they were deleted.

Once the Mexican, German, and black Texans had been subordinated by the Anglo-Celtic Protestant majority, the only threat to the plantation- and ranch-owning elite in Texas came from within the dominant white Southern tribe itself. Poor whites and radicals who joined the Populist and Socialist movements in the late nineteenth and early twentieth centuries terrified the neo-Confederate estab-lishment—particularly because some of them talked of an alliance of poor whites and poor blacks against the rich. The response of the oli-garchy throughout the South was swift, brutal, and effective. In 1890, Mississippi adopted a new constitution that used a poll tax and a lit-eracy test to purge most black voters and to put white voters in the legal majority in the electorate for the first time since the Civil War. Other Southern states imitated Mississippi, including Texas in 1902. Almost all blacks and many low-income whites were effectively stripped of the right to vote.

To the benefit of the white rich, the white poor turned their frus-tration against the mostly poor black population in a wave of lynch-ings that were concentrated in East Texas counties, where landowning blacks competed with large numbers of poor whites. The Ku Klux Klan underwent a renaissance in the early twentieth century in Texas, the South, and parts of the Midwest, opposing a diffuse range of alleged threats to the Anglo-Celtic Protestant way of life, including racial equality, political liberalism, socialism and communism, evolu-tionary theory, secular humanism, and alleged conspiracies by Jews and Catholics. The membership of the Klan, the Baptist Church, and the Democratic Party overlapped.

Hardly any Europeans immigrated to Texas during the period of mass European immigration between the Civil War and World War I. Like the rest of the South, Texas was poor, violent, and known for its hostility to foreigners. Nor was there much immigration from other parts of the United States, with the exception of a few Midwestern-ers who moved to the wheatfields of the Panhandle and to the heav-ily Mexican-Texan "Valley," where they formed a small Midwestern middle-class and business elite. Most immigration to Texas between the Civil War and World War II was from the South, so that the South-ern character of the state was reinforced rather than diluted by newcomers.

———————————

By World War I, a pattern had emerged in Texas that would remain intact until the Civil Rights Revolution, although it would be shaken by the New Deal. Texas was what sociologists call a *Herrenvolk,* or master-race democracy—a democracy in which the ethnic majority controls the government and uses it to repress ethnic, racial, and religious minorities. Blacks and many poor whites were disenfranchised by literacy tests, poll taxes, and intimidation. The Democratic Party monopolized state and local offices. The number of Republican voters was tiny—and their votes were even sometimes discarded.* As in other one-party Democratic states, the Democratic primary was the actual election, as the candidate who emerged from that usually won, except in the case of a primary that resulted in a run-off election. One-party politics maximized the leverage of the Solid South in national politics—and of Texas in its own right. In the early twentieth century, Lloyd Bentsen, Sr., the father of the Texas senator, visited R. B. Creager, the state chairman of the Republican Party:

> I told Mr. Creager that I wanted to join the Republican party since my daddy had always been a rock-ribbed Republican in South Dakota. He said, "Young man, do you want to do what's best for Texas?" I said I did. And he told me, "You go back to Mission and join the Democratic party, because what's best for Texas is for every state in the union to have a two-party system and for Texas to be a one-party state. When you have a one-party state, your men stay in Congress longer and build up seniority."[6]

Although there were moderate and even liberal Democrats—and a faction of New Deal Democrats that became important, beginning in the 1930s—conservatives dominated the Texas Democratic Party. The most successful political formula in Texas during the Confederate Century consisted of the folksy Scots-Irish hillbilly populist style in politics enlisted in the service of the commodity economics and racial hierarchy favored by the Anglo-American ruling class of the Deep South.

The Populist movement of the 1880s and 1890s, like the evanescent Socialist movement that succeeded it in the Plains and Southwest, had represented a genuine threat to the oligarchy in Texas and the

---

*"Hell, we threw every third Republican vote away on account of it was 'illegible,'" a Democratic vote counter from Starr County once told me, referring to a period as recent as the 1960s.

other Deep South states. By contrast, the populist politics of the period between World War I and the 1960s in Texas was a harmless, licensed populism that entertained the public without threatening the perquisites of the small number of families that ran the state as their collective fiefdom. Many of the Populist politicians, like the two-term governor James Ferguson (1871–1944) and his wife Miriam (1871–1944), who was also a two-term governor—better known as "Pa" and "Ma" Ferguson—were corrupt figures who had no serious programs, even if they enacted a few reforms.

The compatibility of pseudo-populism and the traditionalism of the Texan oligarchy is illustrated by the career of W. Lee O'Daniel (1890–1969), who was governor of Texas between 1938 and 1941 and U.S. senator from Texas from 1941 until his retirement in 1949. Born in Ohio and raised in Kansas, he moved to Fort Worth at the age of 35 and became sales manager of a flour company, Burrus Mills. O'Daniel turned the company's radio advertising spots into his own radio show, in which he promoted Christianity and Burrus Mills flour and performed songs he wrote with his own band, the Light Crust Doughboys. Having become president of the Fort Worth Chamber of Commerce in 1933, O'Daniel ran for governor in 1938, opportunistically invoking some of the themes of the New Deal, including the need for Social Security and industrialization in Texas. It was during this campaign that he became known as "Pappy" O'Daniel, thanks to the commercial theme song of his "Hillbilly Flour Hour":

> I like Mountain Music,
> Good ole Mountain Music,
> Played by a real hillbilly band.
> I like bread and biscuits,
> Big, white fluffy biscuits,
> Hillbilly flour makes 'em grand.
> So while we sing and play
> And try to make folks happy,
> We hope you'll say,
> Please pass the biscuits, pappy!

A campaign song in 1940 contained the following stanza:

No use to have a grouch
Or even have a frown
For everybody's happy
When Pappy comes to town.[7]

As governor, O'Daniel allowed business lobbies to run the state as they pleased. Now and then he sang songs for the state legislature. He stacked the Regents of the University of Texas with reactionaries and supported them when they fired Homer Rainey, the president of the University of Texas, for subversive acts such as permitting students to read John Dos Passos's novel *USA* and tolerating liberals on the faculty, and he prevailed on the statehouse to pass an anti-union bill, the O'Daniel Anti-Violence Act, which was too extreme even for the conservative state judiciary. In a special Senate election in 1941, with the help of voter fraud in East Texas, O'Daniel defeated FDR's candidate, the young Congressman Lyndon Johnson, and went to Washington.

Although his father had been a veteran of the Union Army, O'Daniel became the embodiment of Southern conservatism. Mindful of the popularity of FDR among ordinary Texans, O'Daniel had pretended now and then to be a Roosevelt supporter. For example, in 1940, he had claimed that he had uncovered a secret fifth column in Texas and informed the president, a lie that helped him to get reelected. But in 1944, O'Daniel conspired with the Texas Regulars, a group of right-wing Democrats, including his successor as governor Coke Stevenson, who plotted to prevent Roosevelt's reelection by siphoning away votes from the Democrats to a third party. The cabal was defeated by the Texas Loyalists, a faction of pro-Roosevelt Democrats led by Johnson. In his last years, like many Texan conservatives, O'Daniel ranted against racial integration and imaginary communist conspiracies.*

As the example of "Pappy" O'Daniel suggests, the Texan conservatives and their fellow Southern conservatives had mixed feelings

---

*There were genuine, if small-scale, Moscow-controlled spy networks in the United States, but none of the Southern conservatives ever discovered any; they were more interested in smearing New Deal liberalism and the civil rights movement by association with communism.

about the New Deal. An alliance of local reformers and the federal government like this had not existed since the end of Reconstruction, and it was worrisome. The response of Southern conservatives was mixed. Some joined the New Deal and used their influence to dilute its potential radicalism, while supporting federal subsidies to Southern industries and government entities. Conservative Texans in the New Deal coalition included FDR's vice-president, John Nance "Cactus Jack" Garner (who turned against FDR in the late 1930s), and Jesse Jones, the Houston banker and businessman who was head of the powerful Reconstruction Finance Corporation (RFC). Conservative Democrats in Congress promoted New Deal legislation that benefited Southern business elites, while blocking or watering down provisions that helped the white and black poor and working class. For example, Southern congressmen were careful to exempt domestic and agricultural workers—categories that included most black Southerners—from protective labor laws. Federal housing programs were applied on a racially discriminatory basis, so that a generation of black Americans were unable to obtain the basic asset of most post-Depression families, a house.

Many conservatives in Texas and other parts of the South rejected the New Deal in its entirety. The hatred many Northeastern patricians had for Roosevelt, whom they considered a class traitor, was nothing compared to the hatred of Southern oligarchs for the former New York governor. They were appalled that Roosevelt was continuing the transformation of the Democratic Party from the party of minimal government, states' rights, and white supremacy into the party of state intervention in the economy and egalitarian social reform.

Between 1938 and the mid-1950s, the Texan right rebelled in a counter-revolution against the New Deal and the early civil rights movement. The uneasy coalition among Texan modernists and Texan conservatives in support of some economic modernization projects ended in bitter warfare. Because Texas was a one-party Democratic state, the battle took the form of an intra-party struggle among the Texas Regulars (a faction of conservative Democrats who sought to deny Roosevelt reelection in 1944) and the Texas Loyalists, pro-Roosevelt Democrats who actually belonged to two distinct but overlapping groups—centrist New Deal liberals like Lyndon Johnson and Sam Rayburn and a small and weak liberal left consisting of white urban professionals, labor organizers, and black and Latino civil rights activists.

The counter-revolutionary right in Texas used every smear tactic available against moderate and liberal Democrats. The Texas Regulars and "Shivercrats," followers of Texas Governor Allan Shivers, defended white supremacy and claimed that labor unions were part of a plot to bring communism to Texas. One of the most strenuous red-baiters was Texan Congressman Martin Dies, the head of the House Un-American Activities Committee (HUAC), who named more names of suspected subversives than Senator Joseph McCarthy did. Some of the accusations that Dies made were plausible; for example, he claimed that, while his hillbilly band was playing, "Pappy" O'Daniel was trying to decide what to say next.[8] Later, Joseph McCarthy became a folk hero among conservative Texans. A number of them pooled contributions of one to one hundred dollars to buy a Cadillac for the Wisconsin Senator as a wedding gift.[9]

Seeking an unprecedented third term as governor in 1954, Shivers smeared his opponent in the primary, the liberal Ralph Yarborough (who joined Johnson in the U.S. Senate between 1957 and 1970, when he was defeated by the conservative Democrat Lloyd Bentsen). Shivers appealed to Confederate states'-rights ideology by claiming the sovereignty of the state of Texas, rather than the federal government, over offshore oil resources. The communist background of some CIO organizers in the Gulf Coast town of Port Arthur gave Shivers and the Texan right the opportunity to claim that Yarborough and other liberals wanted Texas to be taken over by the Communist Party, "the ADA, the NAACP, and all the rest of that kind." The cynicism of the Texan oligarchy is evident in a memo to Shivers written by one of his campaign managers, Weldon Hart:

> You badly need a burning issue for the last 10 days, such as segregation furnished in your closing First Primary drive. . . .
> The "outside labor bosses" haven't scared the voters much, as too many of them either don't believe the threat is real or don't see how they are involved either way.

I submit for your consideration a doublepronged program to
bring the labor issue closer to home by:

1. Using the Port Arthur story as a threat to businessmen
   everywhere;
2. Using the farm labor unionization threat, especially in
   West Texas.

Hart warned Shivers that "because of your personal involvements" the
governor might "be open to counterattack." He was referring to the fact
that Shivers was a rich landowner from the Anglo-dominated Rio
Grande Valley of South Texas, where his overseers exploited non-union-
ized Mexican-American labor, including, no doubt, many illegal aliens.[10]

The economic policy favored by the conservative Democrats who
ruled Texas during the first two-thirds of the twentieth century
advanced the interests of owners of large, commodity-exporting enterprises like Allen Shivers and their partners, investors outside of the
state. Having failed during the Civil War to realize its ambition of leaving the United States to become a formally sovereign but economically dependent resource colony of London, the South, from its
perspective, achieved the next best thing: it became a resource colony
of New York. The terms that were negotiated in the 1870s were unfa-
vorable to the Southern white and black majority, but very favorable
to the Southern rich, who were given a free hand by the Northeastern elite in crushing dissent within their region, in return for becoming reliable suppliers of cotton, cattle, and (later) oil and gas.

"By 1900," one historian writes, "the economy of Texas, in terms
of the state's leading components, had become integrated thoroughly
with that of the rest of the United States on the colonial basis of sup-
plying raw materials to the industrialized sectors and importing manufactured products."[11] During the Depression, the liberal Southern
sociologist Howard Odum observed that the South as a whole was
"essentially colonial in its economy" and had "the general status of an
agricultural country engaged in trade with industrial countries."[12] The
resource-colony economy of Texas was not a self-contained, premodern subsistence economy, but an outward-oriented, commodity-

exporting economy that played an important role in the national and global industrial system by complementing rather than competing with the manufacturing economies. The first industrial revolution in the nineteenth century produced a demand for cotton and cattle, to clothe and feed workers in urban, industrial areas; the second industrial revolution in the twentieth century produced a demand for oil and gas.

From the beginning, the "commodity patch"—the sum of agricultural and mineral enterprises in Texas—has been only partly Texan. According to one historian, through most of the twentieth century, "three-fourths of Texas oil was owned by 'Wall Street,' in the broad usage of that term. Even the so-called independents, such as Humble Oil Company and Magnolia Refinery, were branches of Standard Oil of New Jersey. Also, a low percentage of oil stock was owned by Texans."[13] The ownership of sulfur mines, agribusiness concerns, and other commodity-sector enterprises was also shared by Texan capitalists with their foreign allies and sponsors. The absentee owners of much of the natural wealth of Texas were not necessarily unenlightened, but at best they had no personal interest in the social conditions in a state in which they did not live and may never have visited. Native capital there tended to come from the commodity sector, and to be reinvested in it. For example, "cotton banks" in Texas like Houston's Anderson, Clayton and Company helped to finance the oil industry.[14]

The description of Southern cities in 1874 by a European visitor, Friedrich Ratzel, applied as well, until around World War II, to Houston or Galveston, important ports on the Gulf of Mexico, or Dallas and Fort Worth, which were inland port cities on overland trade routes:

> The general character of Southern cities [is] . . . very different from their Northern and Western counterparts. . . . The commerce of this area is still not connected to any industrial activity to speak of. For that reason, besides the big merchants here there are no big industrialists, no skilled workers, nor a vigorous white working class of any size worth mentioning. The shopkeepers and handworkers cannot make up for the lack of these hearty classes that create civilization and wealth. Therefore, . . . this society has an incomplete, half-developed profile like that which one tends

to associate with the industry-less large cities of predominantly agricultural countries. In this regard, New Orleans, Mobile, Savannah, and Charleston look more like Havana and Veracruz than, say, Boston or Portland.[15]

The discovery and development of the Texas oil fields only reinforced the bias of the Texas political class toward the commodity sector. Rich landowners moved easily into new roles as rich leaseholders and shareholders of oil companies. Like farming and ranching, the oil business, as a business, was based on land ownership. Some of the old cotton-farming and cattle-ranching families of Texas, joined by wealthy northern immigrants like George Bush, Sr., grew easily into the oil-patch elite. The strategy was the same: buy land, and then use market power or political influence to try to rig the prices of the commodities on top of it or the minerals underneath it. Until OPEC replaced it, the Texas Railroad Commission—originally established to protect Texan producers from unfair railroad practices—unfairly rigged the world price for oil from the 1920s until the 1970s.[16]

The attitude of the Texas oil men, presumably shared with their out-of-state investor allies, toward the natural environment was the same as that of the big farmers and ranchers. Nature was to be used up for a profit and then discarded. Cotton monoculture ruined the river-bottom soil. Overgrazing ruined the prairie soil. Oil wells and water wells for agricultural irrigation depleted resources that could not be replaced. Nothing could be more preposterous than the claim of traditional Southerners that they "love the land." Having seized it from Spain (Florida), Mexico (Texas), and the American Indians, they plundered and exhausted it—and the successful ones moved on, to new fields, fresh pastures, or untapped oil and gas leases. The mentality of the traditional elite in the rural South is that of a real estate speculator, not a peasant farmer who treasures and improves his modest piece of the earth in order to pass it down to his heirs.

More to the point, it is the attitude of a certain kind of aristocrat. Texan business is often thought of as capitalism in its rawest form. Capitalist Texas may be, but it is not and never has been bourgeois.

Bourgeois capitalism is what one usually thinks of when discussing capitalism. It is the capitalism of the Dutch burghers and the British factory owners, of the Yankee tycoons of the Gilded Age, and of their counterparts in Imperial Germany. Bourgeois capitalism has come in two versions: mercantile capitalism, based on long-distance trading, which flourished from the late Middle Ages in Europe until the advent of the industrial revolution in the eighteenth and nineteenth centuries; and industrial capitalism. The industrial capitalists who owned steel factories and car factories, like the earlier mercantile capitalists who got rich by selling Asian spices, African slaves, or West Indian or Brazilian tobacco or cotton, were bourgeois in countries like Britain and the regions like the American Northeast that pioneered industrialism.

All bourgeoisies are capitalist, but all capitalists are not bourgeois. The term "bourgeois" is often used as a synonym for capitalist or middle class, but this is a mistake. There are middle classes that are not capitalist, but comprised of educated professionals or civil servants. German scholars correctly distinguish between the *Besitzbürgertum,* or propertied bourgeoisie (business owners and industrialists), and the *Bildungsbürgertum,* or educated/credentialed bourgeoisie (professors, lawyers, doctors, ministers, civil servants, and military officers). Just as there are middle-class elites that are not capitalist, so there are capitalist elites that are not bourgeois in any meaningful sense. The great landlord families of the American South and Southwest and the West Indies and Latin America have been capitalist. But the fact that one owns property and engages in market transactions does not, in itself, make one bourgeois.

The bourgeois capitalist, as a social type, is as much defined by politics and morality as by economics. The very term "bourgeois" refers to a political fact, not an economic fact—legal status as a burgher or citizen of a free city in medieval or early modern Europe. Between the late Middle Ages and the Renaissance, European city-states in northern Italy and the Low Countries (present-day Belgium and the Netherlands) obtained their independence from popes, emperors, and local aristocrats. Their "burghers" or elite citizens laid the groundwork of modern constitutional, republican government and commercial capitalism at the same time. The fact that European capitalism originated and flourished in republican city-states like those of Renaissance Italy and the Netherlands was no accident. Then as now, capital and capitalists tend to flee from despotic regimes that have the arbitrary power to confiscate their wealth, and to find homes in constitutional states where property and person alike are secure against arbitrary government.

After Spain, with the help of the Inquisition, killed off intellectual and economic freedom in occupied Italy in the sixteenth century, the centers of both capitalist economics and constitutional politics were the Netherlands in the seventeenth-century and Britain and its North American colonies in the eighteenth century. London succeeded Amsterdam as the center of world commerce, only to be superseded in the twentieth century by New York—which, not coincidentally, had been founded by Dutch merchants and had first been named New Amsterdam.

Although the Netherlands, Britain, and the early United States were Protestant societies, Protestantism in itself is not the source of the bourgeois ethic (Max Weber's attempt to link the two was simply incorrect). What is thought of today as the typical bourgeois ethic—an emphasis on profit, thrift, long-term investment, and a willingness to trade with anyone, combined with an emphasis on this world rather than an afterlife and a willingness to experiment rather than be bound by custom—existed as early as the eleventh and twelfth centuries among the nominally Catholic capitalists of Italy and other parts of Europe. The bourgeois ethic was defined from the beginning against the aristocratic ethic, the ethic of the European knights. While there was a certain degree of social overlap, the knights—provincial and often primitive landowners who specialized in warfare on behalf of king, Christendom, or their own interests—tended to be the opposites of the new merchant-princes. The knights often commanded vast territories, but seldom ventured beyond them, unless on a Crusade or an expedition of conquest. The merchants, from their tiny walled cities, sent forth, and sometimes led, trading expeditions to the edges of the known world. The knights disdained labor; the burghers prized it. The knights spent their wealth recklessly; the burghers accumulated it. The knights, on encountering foreigners, sought to subjugate them; the burghers wanted to barter. The knights disdained profit and treasured honor; the burghers, although they were not insensible to honor, valued profit more.

It is a fact of immense historic significance—not least to Texas— that the European settlements in most of the western hemisphere were founded not by merchants but by knights like the conquistadors of Spain and the royalist aristocrats (and, what is pretty much the same, the would-be aristocrats) of Virginia. The association of the Americas with freedom and democracy is a relatively new development; from the time of Columbus until the American Revolution, many Europeans thought of "the plantations" in the western hemisphere as frightening, primitive places characterized by slavery and other forms of involuntary servitude. During this long era, the historian Raimondo Luraghi writes,

> however different the external conditions, both Americas, from French Canada down to Spanish South America, showed striking structural similarities. The exceptions were New England and the so-called Middle Colonies (New York, New Jersey, Pennsylvania), which were bourgeois and capitalist. Everywhere the foundation of society was agriculture, mainly based on large-scale land property; everywhere a distinctive single-crop or single-staple economy prevailed (furs in French Canada; tobacco, rice, and indigo in southern English colonies; sugar in the Caribbean and in Brazil). Everywhere . . . slavery was the dominant labor system; everywhere the social body was ruled by a particular class, agricultural, paternalistic, more similar in its social connotations to European nobility than to the bourgeoisie, with whom, indeed, it had nothing in common.[17]

The Southern oligarchy—in its various historic incarnations, ranging from enlightened slaveowners of Virginia like Jefferson and Madison to reactionary West Texas oil men born to family wealth—is a genuine aristocracy. The members of the Anglo-Southern "chivalry" who, in the nineteenth century, compared one another to Bayard, the *chevalier peur et sans reproche*, were not pretentious frauds who had read too many books by Sir Walter Scott. They were the real thing: a hereditary ruling class with a premodern mentality whose power rested in ownership of land and domination of politics and the military. They were first cousins of the British aristocracy and distant cousins of the Prussian Junkers, the Spanish creole elite, and the Russian service nobility. For centuries in their English-speaking section of tropical America they rode horses, fought duels, and were waited on by hordes of slaves or servants from birth until death. They were usually better at spending money than at making it. They were not bourgeois.

Neither are their lineal and cultural descendants. The clownish arrivistes who symbolize Texas in the popular imagination distract attention from the tasteful, educated, courteous, and collectively ruthless members of the social elite who simultaneously dominate business, politics, and culture in the state. The typical Texan oligarch is not a hillbilly who struck oil and wears expensive python-skin boots, but someone who inherited family wealth, which usually originated in land a generation or two back. Appended to this hereditary elite, and sharing its lifestyle to the degree that they can, is a deferential and subservient professional class made up of corporate executives, bankers, and lawyers who do not challenge the oligarchy because they aspire to join it. In Texas, professions like law and banking have been as nepotistic as business. This is not a bourgeois elite, nor is it a meritocratic credentialed "overclass." The term "gentry" is more accurate.

Both the hereditary rich and their professional-class retainers in the broad gentry typically have been well-educated, in the Ivy League or the good state universities like UT or SMU. They are more likely to be Episcopalians or Methodists than Baptists, although that is changing as Baptists become more upscale and cede lower-class Protestant enthusiasm to Pentecostalists and other sects. The oligarchs are well-traveled, with a fondness for vacations in Europe, particularly Britain (like all elite Southerners, they are Anglophiles). Many are distant cousins of upper-class Louisianans, Alabamians, Mississippians, Georgians, and Virginians, and many can trace their genealogy back to British antecedents who immigrated to the Southern colonies. Their homes are tasteful suburban mansions or country houses in Highland Park, Dallas, or River Oaks, Houston, or Westlake Hills, Austin, decorated with fine art in one of the two prestigious transatlantic styles—traditional classicism or abstract modernism. While they tend to be conservative in their social attitudes, they would consider it vulgar to express overt racial or religious bigotry. As individuals, they are often open-minded and magnanimous; as a class, they are almost always intolerant and selfish. While opposing more than minimal taxation and public services, they give generously to the elite universities that their children attend and to upper-crust cultural institutions like symphony orchestras and fine arts museums.

Although they may look like members of the old-stock Protestant business class of the Northeast, Midwest, and West Coast, the oligarchs of Texas do not think like them. The mentality of the traditional Texan businessman is that of the premodern "seigneurial" elite which, according to Luraghi, included not only the Southern slaveowners but also the British "Nabobs" of the West Indies, the Mexican *hacendados*, and the Brazilian plantation owners. It is not an industrial capitalist mind-set at all, but the mentality of the Spanish conquistador, who dreamed of quickly acquiring fabulous wealth by plundering precious metals rather than by patient effort.

Oil is a mineral, like gold and silver. It is no coincidence that much of Texas folklore revolves around hunts for lost treasure. Often in the legends the mine was first found by Spanish conquistadors and then forgotten—a motif that links the Anglo-Southern fortune hunter to his aristocratic Spanish predecessor. The Southern planters and ranchers, like their Spanish and Latin American counterparts, thought it was more honorable, and certainly more exciting, to find, or steal, a gold or silver mine than to spend years devising more efficient ways to utilize the resources that they already controlled.

One of the most popular tales in the impoverished folklore of Anglo-Celtic Texas is the story that the famous knife-fighter Jim Bowie discovered a lost Spanish silver mine before he was killed in the battle of the Alamo. Cortes and Pizarro and Coronado and other Spanish thugs dreamed of American Indian treasure; Bowie and other Anglo-Celtic Texan adventurers in turn dreamed of Spanish treasure. Two of the Texas folklorist J. Frank Dobie's most popular books of Texana, *Coronado's Children* and *Apache Gold and Yaqui Silver,* were collections of legends about lost hoards of Indian or Spanish treasure.

When Nelson and Bunker "Bunky" Hunt, children of the Dallas oil man H. L. Hunt, tried to corner the world silver market in 1980, they created a legend of their own in the spirit of the tradition. And then there is white gold, the greatest source of wealth in Texas before the discovery of oil; as one authority on the history of the Texas economy observes, "even with modern production techniques, cotton is a 'gambler's crop.'"[18]

While Spanish conquistadors were torturing Indians in Texas (originally called the New Philippines by the Spanish) and other parts of the western hemisphere to learn the location of rumored gold and silver mines and mythical treasure cities like Cibola and Quivira, their Dutch subjects were fighting a war of independence from Spain, which they won partly thanks to their flooding of the dikes their ingenuity and industry had created. Before James Watt perfected the steam engine, the Dutch had already pioneered the industrial revolution by using windmills to power partly mechanized factories. Unlike their imperial Spanish overlords and the Anglo-American "chivalry" of the plantation South and the West Indies, the Dutch did not have a servile population to do their work. They made a virtue of necessity and invented modern technological civilization. Centuries later, in the Texas Hill Country, where industrious German families were known as "the Dutch" to their Anglo-Celtic neighbors, water-power instead of wind-power was used to create a technological economy in the hills west of Austin which, by the 1990s, were known as the Silicon Hills because of the Austin computer industry.

The confusion of capitalism with gambling on the part of the Texan oligarchs, while it results in some spectacular fortunes and memorable parties, also produces titanic bankruptcies and business failures. It is significant, perhaps, that the epochal collapses of Enron and Worldcom in 2002 occurred to companies headquartered, respectively, in Houston and Clinton, Mississippi—and that each company's growth strategy combined good-old-boy politicking with bluffing and swindling on a heroic scale. The Texas real estate boom of the 1980s, too, was a typical speculative bubble augmented by unethical business practices.

Just as alien as thrift and efficiency to the Southern aristocratic mind is the concept of invention. The "Yankee inventor"—Edison,

Ford—is a familiar figure. A disproportionate number of the native-born innovators in the American computer industry have been middle-class white Protestants from the Yankee-settled Midwest or Pacific Coast. One of the few famous Southern inventors was Cyrus McCormick, a Virginian, and his invention, the McCormick Reaper, was not wanted in the pre–Civil War South because slaves were cheaper than machines. (McCormick made a fortune in the North, where high wages among free workers created an incentive for mechanized agriculture.)

Once the pre-bourgeois, aristocratic mentality of the Texan/Southern oligarchy is understood, the legendary flamboyance of the Texan rich can be viewed in a new light. Northeasterners often assume that the big spenders must be gauche social climbers. But the hillbilly with oil on his land was the exception rather than the rule (if only because such people tended to be swindled by better-educated businessmen, the myth of the canny yokel notwithstanding). Showing off is part of the old-money tradition—not only in Texas but in other parts of the South, where patrician families whose social status is secure compete to lavish money on debutante balls, weddings, Mardi Gras floats, and mansions.*

The flamboyance of many rich Texans, and their Southern kin, is that of an upper class that feels no guilt about its wealth and privileges. It is that of an aristocrat from a British-American culture that was untouched by bourgeois and Puritan influences during its formative years in the seventeenth and eighteenth centuries. Our notions of the gentleman are formed by the patricians of the Northeast and the British aristocracy of the late nineteenth century. In the Northeastern United States, arrivistes were shown how to behave by a bourgeois patriciate with a stern Puritan tradition. In Britain, the aristocracy had reformed itself in the nineteenth century. Frightened by the French Revolution, pressured from below by a dissenting Protestant middle class, and schooled in notions of self-sacrificing

---

*I know of one family of wealthy Texans, rich for generations, who greeted a member of the West Coast branch of the family at the San Antonio airport by hiring a Mexican-American mariachi band to serenade him as he got off the plane.

public service at Thomas Arnold's Rugby and other elite schools, the Victorian aristocrats adopted a pose of discipline, modesty, and sobriety, at least in public. But before the mid-Victorian rise in public piety and gentility, British aristocrats had been flamboyant, hard-drinking, whoring, shooting, hunting, and dueling "barbarians"—that is the term that Matthew Arnold used for the British upper classes.

The Nieman Marcus department store in Dallas, Texas, is world-famous for its startling contributions to what Thorstein Veblen, a Norwegian-American intellectual with a typically Scandinavian disdain for excess, called the culture of "conspicuous consumption." One year the Nieman Marcus catalogue offered matching his and her giraffes; another year, his and her submarines. This is not the world of self-made Gilded Age tycoons like Carnegie or Jay Gould, who, in amassing European art treasures in personal palaces, were trying to be respectable. True aristocrats are so secure in their status that they do not need to earn respectability, and can choose to be interesting. His and her submarines! This is not the crudeness of a rich hillbilly, but the flamboyance of an aristocrat uninhibited by bourgeois modesty or liberal guilt about wealth, the magnificence of a grandee who was born on top and intends to stay there.

THREE

Philip Dru, Texan

In the fall of 1912, a novel entitled *Philip Dru: Administrator* attracted attention in the United States. Interest among reviewers was stimulated by the description of the anonymous author as "a man prominent in political councils." Some speculated that the book had been written by former President Theodore Roosevelt.

Philip Dru is a Progressive political manifesto disguised as a work of fiction. The action of the book takes place in what at the time of its publication was the near future, between 1920 and 1935. Philip Dru, a Kentucky-born army officer, abandons his military career after suffering from eye problems while stationed on the Texas-Mexican border. His idealism inspires him to move to New York's tenement district on the Lower East Side. Here he rents a room from Ben Levinsky, the kindly survivor of a massacre of Jews in Warsaw, and begins a new career as a muck-raking Progressive journalist, writing articles and delivering lectures about the evils of social inequality and industrial inefficiency.

When the scheme of two titans of industry and finance to use campaign donations and bribes to control the federal government accidentally becomes known to the public, civil war breaks out in the United States. Philip Dru—now General Dru—leads the armed forces of the patriotic insurgents, who are based in the West and South, against the forces of the plutocratic government, which has its greatest support in the industrial Northeast. The Progressive hero is literally a man on horseback: "In that hell storm of lead and steel Dru sat upon his horse unmoved." In a single cataclysmic battle in which

40,000 government troops and 23,000 rebel troops are killed, the
patriots defeat the plutocracy.

> General Dru now called a conference of his officers and
> announced his purpose of assuming the powers of a dictator, dis-
> tasteful as it was to him, and, as he felt it might also be, to the
> people. He explained that such a radical step was necessary, in
> order to quickly purge the government of those abuses that had
> arisen, and give to it the form and purpose for which they had
> fought. . . . He then issued an address to his army proclaiming
> himself *"Administrator of the Republic."*

During his seven-year protectorate, this Progressive American
Cromwell enfranchises women and establishes universal suffrage
"without distinction of race, color or sex," reforms the federal and
state constitutions and courts, fixes the Railroad Problem, establishes
the federal incorporation of businesses, mandates the representation
of organized labor on corporate boards, and codifies the laws. In
foreign relations, he sends troops to Mexico to impose order and
checks German and Japanese ambitions by means of an Anglo-
American alliance: "The American Navy at the close of Philip Dru's
wise administration was second only to that of England, and together
the two great English speaking nations held in their keeping the peace
and commercial freedom of the Seven Seas." His work done, he weds
the love of his life, Gloria Strawn, and departs into voluntary exile, literally sailing into the sunset from San Francisco Bay.

Philip Dru is not a great or even a competent work of fiction. Like
the far more accomplished political novels of Benjamin Disraeli, it is
a tract wrapped in an allegory. Much of it consists of lectures on political economy and contemporary social problems delivered by the hero
to his adoring and endlessly patient girlfriend, Gloria. She is the only
character in the novel with whom the reader can sympathize: "Long
before Philip had finished speaking, Gloria saw that he had forgotten
her presence."[1]

The author of *Philip Dru*, the world eventually learned, was
Edward Mandell House (1858–1938). He was indeed a "man prominent in political councils." After serving as an influential power bro-

ker in Texas politics, House became a friend, confidante, and aide to President Woodrow Wilson, until their friendship broke down after World War I. Although he had never served in the military, House was universally known by the title "Colonel House," an honorific bestowed upon him by Texas Governor James Stephen Hogg, after he helped Hogg win the governorship in 1892. In the 1930s, Franklin Roosevelt, who as assistant secretary of the navy during the Wilson administration had known House, enlisted him to help him win the Democratic presidential nomination. Once in the White House, FDR corresponded with the Texan, who never, however, had influence comparable to that which he exercised during the Wilson years.

Nothing in House's biography explains his maturation into a leading American Progressive. Born in Houston to a rich merchant, banker, and plantation owner, House was an indifferent student at Cornell. Returning to Texas, he managed the family cotton plantations, speculated in real estate, and built himself a magnificent mansion in Austin, before building up a faction in Texas politics called "our crowd." He dabbled in the oil business after oil was discovered at Spindletop in 1901 and invested in a Texas railroad. Until the early 1900s, there was little to distinguish him from any other member of the small upper class in Texas. But he had traveled repeatedly to Europe, beginning in his childhood, and spent more time in the Northeast as he grew older.[2] House found a kindred spirit in New Jersey's Governor Wilson, another Southern-born politician and intellectual with national ambitions. The day after his election as president, Wilson traveled to Bermuda, where he read *Philip Dru*.[3]

Since the 1930s, conservative and libertarian conspiracy theorists have claimed that House's science-fiction novel was a blueprint for the New Deal. In fact, it is less interesting for what it foreshadowed in the administrations of Woodrow Wilson and Franklin Roosevelt than for what it revealed about a strain in Texan political culture that became increasingly important in the twentieth century—in national politics, no less than in state politics.

This strain might be called the Texan modernist tradition. While it departed from the Texan conservative tradition, Texan modernism was not necessarily liberal, in the contemporary sense, in which liberalism is defined by attitudes on social issues like abortion, feminism, homosexuality, and racial preferences. Whether they were liberal, centrist, or conservative in their views on race, sex, and gender, the modernists were the major rivals to the traditionalists in twentieth-century Texas.

These visionary modernizers have included Lyndon Johnson and Sam Rayburn, and, in a later generation, Ross Perot and former National Security Agency director Bobby Ray Inman. Their goal was a modernizing economic and social revolution from above in Texas, and their chosen instrument was state capitalism—civilian or military. They were not socialists, but they were statists. Their logic has been similar to that of leaders in many newly industrializing countries. In a backward rural society, in which most private investment flows to the commodity-exporting sector, the government must lead the way in technological modernization, acting sometimes as both an investor and an entrepreneur. Like Colonel House's hero, most of them combined an enthusiasm for political and social reform and advanced technology with populism and a military ethic in a synthesis that, although not unique to Texas, was particularly pronounced in the Lone Star State.

The Texan modernists included people as different in their views and values as John Connally on the right and Barbara Jordan on the left. But in different ways, they were all heirs of Philip Dru.

———————————

The early development of industrial capitalism by a few societies—entire nations like Britain and regions within large countries like the Northeastern-Midwestern core region in the United States—presented the pre-industrial societies in the rest of the world with two options: they could complement, without challenging, the communities that pioneered industrialism, or they could emulate them and strive to become their equals, if not their rivals.

The easiest option was for a backward region to complement an advanced one. An agrarian, traditional society could remain agrarian and traditional by specializing as a resource colony in a national or global economy. The agrarian country would export tobacco, cotton, wheat, beef, precious metals, or oil to the industrial areas, and import machinery, books, magazines, works of art, scholars, and fashions. The traditional, largely rural way of life—including the deference of the majority to the landed elite, be it the Southern planter class, the Mexican *hacendados*, the West Indian planters, or the Argentine ranchers—would suffer only minimal disturbance as a result of this strategy.

For an agrarian society to compete with an already industrialized nation or region on equal terms was much more difficult. The early industrial cores, like Britain and the American Northeast, had bourgeois capitalists in the form of existing mercantile elites who could easily make the transition from trade-based commercial capitalism to industrialism. Many agrarian regions and countries, while they had property-owners and shopkeepers, had nothing resembling a wealthy, thrifty, industrious, educated bourgeoisie capable of long-range strategy of the British or Dutch or New England Yankee kind. To make matters worse, there was little or no local capital for investment in manufacturing industries and industrial infrastructure. In many agrarian societies, most of the wealth was locked up in the land (and sometimes the slaves) of a small oligarchy of rich families, who were often committed to preserving the agrarian order.

For centuries, business and political elites in advanced manufacturing areas have used a variety of techniques to prevent the industrialization of areas which they have assigned the role of resource colonies. One is political imperialism. When the English conquered Ireland and India, they outlawed the Irish and Indian textile industries. Another is "dumping"—selling products below cost for a time in order to wipe out competitors. John Adams wrote in 1819: "I am old enough to remember the war of 1745, and its end; the war of 1755, and its close; the war of 1775, and its termination; the war of 1812, and its pacification. . . . The British manufacturers, immediately after the peace, disgorged upon us all their stores of merchandise and manufactures, not only without profit, but at certain loss for a time, with the express purpose of annihilating all our manufacturers, and ruining all our manufactories."[4] The British were sometimes brutally candid about their intention to sabotage potential industrial competitors. Following the Napoleonic Wars, which by cutting off transatlantic trade stimulated the growth of American manufacturing, Lord Henry Brougham in 1816 told Parliament: "It is well worthwhile to incur a loss upon the first exportation, in order by the glut, to *stifle in the cradle*, those rising manufactures, in the United States, which the war had *forced* into existence, contrary to the natural course of things."[5] The "natural course of things," according to British politicians and British theorists of free trade, required the United States to supply Britain with agricultural goods and raw materials and to import, rather than make, all of its machinery and manufactured goods.

Another method of keeping peripheral economies locked into the status of commodity-exporting resource colonies involved transportation. In the late nineteenth century, private railroads in the United States whose owners were also investors in Northeastern factories sometimes charged higher prices for in-state shipments of manufactured goods than for shipments across state lines. As a result, a product made in a factory in Texas that was otherwise identical to one manufactured in Pennsylvania would cost a Texan consumer more.

Often bankers in the core industrial areas would only loan money to commodity-sector enterprises in peripheral regions or countries, which were pressured to specialize in their "comparative advantage," defined as commodity production or sometimes manufacturing done by cheap and uneducated labor. In the nineteenth and early twentieth centuries, London bankers might invest in an Argentine railroad to help put Argentine beef on British tables—but they were not going to invest in Argentine factories that might compete with British factories. In the same era, New York bankers might support infrastructure projects that would get Texan cotton or cattle to Northeastern markets—but they were no more interested in factories in Texas than the London bankers were in promoting Argentine industry. (The only significant industry in the South before World War II was the textile industry, which Southern states lured from New England with a "pro-business" climate consisting of anti-labor laws and low wages.)

The experience of William Gibbs McAdoo, who became Woodrow Wilson's secretary of the treasury, was typical. As a young businessman in the 1880s, McAdoo invested in a streetcar in Knoxville, Tennessee. According to Jordan A. Schwarz, "realizing that the success of the line depended upon conversion to electricity, and needing capital for this modernization, McAdoo journeyed north in quest of credit, only to learn that New York bankers were doubtful of the enterprise's profitability. Like other Southern entrepreneurs, he discovered that Wall Street investors preferred putting their funds into regional railroads or raw materials rather than into the development of impoverished Southern consumer markets."[6]

The resentment of many Southerners at dependence on Northern manufacturers for the most basic items of life was memorably expressed in the early twentieth century by Henry Grady, the editor of the *Atlanta Constitution*:

> They buried him in the midst of a marble quarry: they cut through solid marble to make his grave; and yet a little tombstone they put above him was from Vermont. They buried him in the heart of a pine forest, and yet the coffin was imported from Cincinnati. They buried him within touch of an iron mine, and yet the nails in his coffin and the iron in the shovel that dug his grave were imported from Pittsburgh. . . . The South didn't furnish a thing on earth for that funeral but the corpse and the hole in the ground.[7]

Thus, from the very beginnings of the industrial era in Britain in the late eighteenth and early nineteenth centuries, the industrial and financial elites in the early industrializing countries and regions have tended to ally themselves with pre-modern commodity-sector elites in pre-industrial societies—to the frustration and fury of would-be modernizers in the latter. The elites in the manufacturing regions were not evil; as individuals, they were often quite enlightened and progressive. But they sought to make profits for themselves and the shareholders of their companies. The industrialization of peripheral agrarian countries threatened the economic primacy of their businesses and their regions—and the well-being of ordinary people in the periphery was not their responsibility. At the same time, in the periphery itself, the development of local industries and urbanization threatened the social and political primacy of the local landlord elites, who could only shudder when they contemplated the likely consequences of the transformation of illiterate and powerless slaves, serfs, peasants, and yeoman farmers into educated citizens and skilled workers and entrepreneurs.

This explains why, in the first half of the nineteenth century, the British—the most technologically advanced society on the planet—were de facto allies, in the politics of international trade, of the reactionary Southern planters and opponents of the Northeastern industrialists. The British and the Southern planters, for their own reasons, wanted a free-trade policy that would have preserved the United States as a non-industrial source of cotton, beef, and other commodities for the British Empire. The Northeastern industrialists who sought to establish new American industries behind a protective tariff threatened both the industrial elites of Britain and the non-industrial elites of the South. However, once the Northern manufacturers had defeated the South in the Civil War and raised tariffs, the Northeastern capitalists, replacing the British bankers and investors, entered into an alliance with the Southern ruling class. The Southern oligarchs would have political power within their own region, which would be a resource colony of New York and Pittsburgh and Chicago rather than London. The Compromise of 1876—in which the Southern Democrats allowed the Republican Rutherford B. Hayes to become president instead of the Democrat Samuel Tilden after a disputed election, in return for the end of Reconstruction in the South—symbolized this postwar modus vivendi between the Northern capitalists and the Southern landlords.

This alliance of convenience between the Northeastern bourgeoisie and the non-bourgeois Southern oligarchy was opposed by Southern political and business leaders who wanted the South to be a center of industry in its own right. The pro-industrial New South leaders like William McAdoo thought little of the Populist William Jennings Bryan's panaceas of free silver and agrarianism. But like other Southerners and Westerners they could sympathize with the resentment of the Northeast expressed in Vachel Lindsay's classic poem "Bryan, Bryan, Bryan, Bryan." Lindsay imagines the astonishment of the eastern "plutocrats" as they behold "a tribe of wonders coming / To a marching tune" from the West: "Oh, the longhorns from Texas, / The jay hawks from Kansas, / The plop-eyed bugaroo and giant giassicus, / The varmint, chipmunk, bugaboo, / The horned-toad, prairie-dog and ballyhoo. . . . They leaped the Mississippi, blue border of the West, / From the Gulf to Canada, two thousand miles long:—Against the towns of Tubal Cain, / Ah,—sharp was their song." The defeat of Bryan by McKinley in the 1896 presidential election is the defeat of part of the continent by another: "Election night at midnight: / Boy Bryan's defeat. Defeat of western silver. / Defeat of the wheat. . . . Victory of custodians, / Plymouth Rock, / And all that inbred landlord stock. / Victory of the neat. / Defeat of the aspen groves of Colorado valleys, / The blue bells of the Rockies, / And blue bonnets of old Texas, / By the Pittsburg alleys."[8]

The Texan historian Walter Prescott Webb, then a professor at the University of Texas in Austin, expressed similar sentiments in less lyrical terms in his 1937 manifesto *Divided We Stand: The Crisis of a Frontierless Democracy*. Webb wrote: "The closing frontier and the growing corporations—both synonymous with decreasing common opportunity—are offered as mated keys to the recent crisis of the modern world's first great democracy."[9] Between the 1860s and the 1930s, Webb argued, the political control of the Northeast over the conquered South and the territories that had become states in the West had diminished, to be replaced by "economic imperial control." What Webb called the new "feudal system" of industrial capitalism was the result of the monopoly of manufacturing and finance by Northeastern capitalists, to whom workers in the North and members of all classes and races in the South and West were forced to pay direct or indirect tribute. "If I could paint a picture representing the general scene, it would be in the form of a great field stretching from Virginia and Florida westward to the Pacific and from Texas and California northward to Canada, an L-shaped region comprising nearly four-fifths of the country. Here millions of people would be playing a game with pennies, nickels, dimes, and dollars, rolling them northward and eastward where they are being stacked almost to the moon."[10] With tongue in cheek, Webb suggested that one possibility was to recognize the existence of industrial feudalism, so that the great capitalists would have formal obligations to house, feed, and shelter their industrial serfs. "The upper house would be composed of representatives elected from the 200 corporations listed by Berle and Means. The lower house would consist of delegates selected by the various blocs representing small business, farmers, laborers, and perhaps the churches and the schools."[11]

The serious alternative that Webb put forth was a permanent degree of government intervention in the economy. He called for "the adoption of a policy for restoring to all sections and classes of the American democracy a semblance of equal economic opportunity."[12] The major industrial corporations needed to take part in a program of geographic decentralization: "They can now decentralize industry through electric power; they can co-operate more with the government, state and national, if they will; they can more generously pour out their largesses to education in those sections from whence their wealth comes."[13] Webb adduced national security in the age of aerial warfare as an additional reason for decentralization: "Security dictates wider distribution of industrial, financial, and manufacturing cities."[14] To promote the decentralization of industry, Webb suggested the adoption of regional tariffs, to stimulate Southern and Western manufacturing by import substitution. This was too radical an idea even at the height of the New Deal, as Webb admitted: "The suggestion of internal tariff walls is too foreign to our philosophy of government and our whole pattern of thinking to be taken seriously or recommended. But if some southern or western congressman wishes to create a sensation, and attract the attention of every northern manufacturer, he may find his opportunity here."[15]

A more practical policy was regulation of national business in the interests of the peripheral South and West—at the state level as well as the national level. In the 1880s, the railroad system in Texas was carved up in deals between three "foreign" railroad barons: Collis Huntington (the Southern Pacific), Jay Gould (the Missouri Pacific), and Cyrus Holliday (the Atcheson, Topeka, and Santa Fe). The abuses of this cartel inspired the creation of the Texas Railroad Commission during the governorship of James Hogg (1891–1895). The Texas Railroad Commission, the first state commission modeled after the then-new Interstate Commerce Commission, banned railroad ownership of "any commercial, agricultural, mining, or other avocation" and regulated railroad rates to level the playing field for Texan enterprises.[16]

While national and state regulation could prevent Northeastern capitalists from rigging the market in favor of their region, regulation could not supply the capital that the South and the West needed for a modern infrastructure and an indigenous industrial and service sector. The answer was public investment—but the investment capital could not come from Texas itself. In Texas, as in the other Southern and Western states, the rich families who owned most of the agricultural and mining and oil enterprises had little to gain, and much to lose, from the modernization of the state and society, and they used their domination of state politics to ensure that the state government would be minimal, weak, and starved of revenues. Thus, public investment had to come, not from the state government in Austin, but from the federal government in Washington.

Beginning with inauguration day, March 4, 1933, the Texans who wanted to modernize Texas by means of state capitalism financed by the federal government had a friend in Washington, D.C.—a very powerful friend indeed.

———————————

"He was a New Yorker and an Easterner," Lyndon Johnson said of Franklin Delano Roosevelt in 1959. "But one of the first tasks which he set himself was the raising up of the South, economic problem number one, still suffering from the destruction of capital in the War between the States. He was an Easterner and a New Yorker but the second important task he set himself was to bring to the West the electric power, the rural electrification and the water which it needed to grow. And the West and the South will forever love him—and follow where he led."[17]

Today Franklin Roosevelt is usually remembered for Social Security and other social welfare programs, as well for his championship of organized labor. But this image of FDR is misleading, for two reasons. The first is that it makes him seem, in retrospect, more of a left-wing social democrat than he was. Pressured by the left of his party and populists like Huey Long, FDR reluctantly consented to the establishment of Social Security in 1936, on the condition that it be solvent and designed according to "insurance principles." (The present pay-as-you-go Social Security system, threatened by insolvency, in which the young subsidize the old, probably would have horrified him.) He was equally unenthusiastic about sponsoring pro-union legislation. He despised "the dole" for able-bodied citizens, preferring "workfare" projects like the Civilian Conservation Corps (CCC) to welfare checks for non-workers. (Aid to Families with Dependent Children, or AFDC, was intended to help widows and orphans.) FDR was also a late convert to Keynesian economic management, which only became the centerpiece of liberal political economy after his death. And he resisted pressure from the left to support federal anti-lynching laws and civil rights laws, partly because he did not want to alienate Southern white Democrats, but also because, unlike his wife Eleanor, he shared the racial prejudices of most white Americans of his time—a failing illustrated by his support for the internment of Americans of Japanese descent, as well as Japanese nationals, during World War II.

The association of Roosevelt with the welfare state and organized labor is misleading for another reason. When he assumed office in the depth of the Great Depression, the United States was still two countries—an industrialized country, the Northeast, surrounded by a backward agrarian country, the Southern/Western periphery. Roosevelt's task in industrialized America was to get the factories going again by putting money in the pockets of the industrial working class, among other things. But in the South and the West there were hardly any factories and no urban, industrial working class to speak of. These regions had more in common with the Northeast in the 1830s, before it was industrialized, than with the Northeast of the 1930s. Roosevelt had to revive existing industries in the Northeast—and build them from nothing in the South and West.

Seen from the perspective of New York and Cambridge, then, the New Deal looks in retrospect like an American version of European social democracy. But in the context of the continental United States as a whole, the social democratic aspects of the New Deal, confined largely to the industrial Northeast and Midwest, were secondary compared to the state-capitalist developmental projects in the South and the West—bringing agrarian societies, which had been bypassed by the age of steam power, directly into the second industrial era of electricity and internal combustion engines in tractors, trucks, and cars.

When FDR wanted to sum up his proudest domestic achievement as president, he often cited the Tennessee Valley Authority (TVA)—a massive public utility company that built dams to generate electricity for farms, towns, and businesses through much of the South. Today, delegates at a Democratic National Convention would snicker in baffled disbelief if a speaker saluted FDR for his greatest accomplishment: rural electrification. But the symbolic significance of the TVA and similar projects, like the Lower Colorado River Authority (LCRA) in Texas, can hardly be exaggerated. They were thought of, not as mere public utility companies, but as the pilot projects of a new and "futuristic" way of life. Roosevelt and many of his allies and supporters believed that the TVA provided a model for a new kind of technological civilization superior to that of the early industrial era. In 1937, Baker Brownell, a professor at Northwestern University, wrote that the TVA was "building more than a dam. It is building a civilization. The visitor here [at Norris Dam] is looking into the next century."[18]

Power-generating dams were to New Deal state capitalists what steel mills were to communists and what stock exchanges were to the neoliberal free-marketeers of the late twentieth century—not just institutions, but icons. Here is a song in *Power*, a pro-New Deal play of 1937: "All up and down the valley / They heard the great alarm; / The government means business / It's working like a charm / Oh, see them boys a-comin' / Their government they trust / Just hear their hammers ringin' / They'll build that dam or bust."[19] Woody Guthrie provided a somewhat better song in "Roll on, Columbia" (1941): "Roll on, Columbia, roll on, / Roll on, Columbia, roll on, / Your power is turning our darkness into dawn / Roll on, Columbia, roll on."[20]

Unlike mainstream American liberals after World War II, FDR was less concerned with the redistribution of income from one group to another than with using new technology and organizational techniques to develop America's productive resources, both natural and human. He was the heir to a well-developed tradition of Progressive thought which, shorn of utopianism and put into contemporary language, can be summarized as follows.

The first industrial revolution was based on the harnessing of steam power for factories and transportation (railroads, steamships). In the United States, the first industrial revolution had been an economic success but a social disaster. Productive industry was overly concentrated in the Northeast, and wealth was overly concentrated in a plutocratic elite whose members sacrificed production to speculation on Wall Street. The combination of industrial technology with an inhumane and inefficient social organization had produced the nightmares that Lewis Mumford described as "Megalopolis" and "Coketown."

Instead of rejecting modern industry (as many agrarians did) or modern corporations (as socialists did) the leading Progressives and New Deal liberals hoped to harness industrial capitalism and to guide it to promote democratic social and political goals. Their major goal was geographic decentralization of both productive industry and people. Industry, concentrated in the Northeastern manufacturing belt, should be dispersed throughout the country. Population, too, should be dispersed. The working classes living in crowded, unsanitary conditions in the big industrial cities should be encouraged to move to low-density suburbs and villagelike "garden cities." The decentralization of industry and population would tend to promote both equality among regions and equality among classes in the United States. The United States should no longer be a collection of resource-producing regions functioning as colonies of a single industrial region, the Northeast. Instead, the country would become a federation of equal regions, each with a mix of manufacturing and agriculture. And as the population left the crowded industrial cities of the Northeast for small, spacious, planned communities, both in the Northeast and in the South and West, the wages of the urban workers who remained would rise.

It was assumed that there would be no significant immigration to the United States in the future. The New Deal era coincided with the era of immigration restriction between the 1920s and the 1960s, when the government deliberately kept immigration low by laws of which FDR approved. In the 1920s and 1930s, FDR and other liberal planners did not foresee that, beginning in the late twentieth century, massive new waves of impoverished and poorly educated immigrants would replace the Americans who left the big cities, depressing the wages of low-skilled workers and re-creating slums, sweatshops, immigrant-fed ethnic voting machines, and other evils that population dispersal was intended to cure.

FDR explained his views about the dispersal of immigrants in 1925 to readers of the *Macon Telegraph,* whose editor, a friend of his, was owner of the Warm Springs spa that FDR bought and converted into a health facility for his fellow victims of polio. The future president rejected nativist bigotry (at least toward European immigrants, the only kind whom America's racist immigration laws permitted to become citizens): "Incidentally, we lack a sense of humor and of proportion if we forget that not so very long ago we were immigrants ourselves. . . . Don't forget that some of the most backward and ignorant sections of the United States in the Northern and Southern States, are sections populated almost exclusively with so-called 'pure American stock.'" But he also wrote: "Taking it by and large, I agree that for a good many years to come European immigration should remain greatly restricted. We have, unfortunately, a great many thousand foreigners who got in here and who must be digested. For fifty years the United States ate a meal altogether too large—much of the food was digestible, but some of it was almost poisonous." Roosevelt told his Southern readers that "we can help this digestive process by encouraging these foreigners to break away from their little foreign groups in our large cities. Many of them, in our cities, come of good, sound stock and would make thoroughly acceptable neighbors in the farming communities. We would be helping not only them, but ourselves, also." FDR praised Canada because its "policy is to prevent large groups of foreign born from congregating in any one locality. In other words, they seek distribution of their immigrants throughout every portion of Canada. . . . If, twenty-five years ago, the United States had adopted a policy of this kind, we would not have the huge foreign sections which exist in so many of our cities."[21] The decentralization of the American population, then, would promote the assimilation of immigrants and accelerate the dissolution of foreign diaspora sub-cultures, which were considered threats to national unity by Roosevelt and like-minded Progressives.

The chief instrument by which the government would promote economic and demographic decentralization would be infrastructure projects taking advantage of the key technologies of the second indus-trial revolution: electricity (hydroelectric dam networks) and the internal combustion engine (highways for cars and trucks). New Dealers often talked about their third way between laissez-faire capi-talism and state socialism as "planning," but the contemporary asso-ciation of this term with socialism is misleading. While they experimented with production quotas in some sectors of the economy like agriculture, Soviet-style economic planning was not what they had in mind. Rather, by planning, the New Deal liberals—at least the less utopian among them—meant a flexible and eclectic combination of zoning, public works, and programs for the provision of public credit that would act as the catalyst for private enterprises to develop certain regions of the country, particularly in the backward South and West, in a desired direction.

In this project, Texans in both Washington and Austin were among the most important leaders. Sam Rayburn championed the New Deal in the House, where in 1936 he became the longest-serving speaker in U.S. history. Wright Patman, like Rayburn a rural Baptist from a poor district in East Texas, had sponsored a resolution to condemn the Ku Klux Klan when he had served in the state legislature in the 1920s; elected to the U.S. Congress, he served for forty-seven years as an ardent New Deal populist. Lyndon Johnson went from being a congressional aide to a congressman in his own right in 1937 at 28, after having been the Texan state director of the National Youth Administration (NYA). A favorite of Roosevelt, the young Texan entered into an alliance with Alvin Wirtz, an Austin lawyer and power broker in state politics, to create a Texan version of the TVA—the LCRA, a state-chartered public utility subsidized by the federal government.

This team of Texan modernists worked closely with their counterparts in other Southern as well as Western states that sought federal aid in industrial development, including California and Oregon. In the 1930s, Rayburn told James Rowe, a young Democratic lawyer from Montana, "Jim, you know, your state reminds me a great deal of Texas. I think in about another generation you will be as civilized as we are."[22]

Civilizing the American frontier required promotion of the fine arts as well as industry. To the project of decentralizing American industry and the American population, many New Deal era progressives joined a corollary project of cultural decentralization. The arts and architecture, they believed, instead of being monopolized by tiny, fashionable cliques of wealthy dilettantes, gallery owners, and museum curators in a few coastal cities, should be interwoven with the lives of all Americans.

In the second half of the twentieth century, the most prestigious liberal intellectuals were residents of New York City or Cambridge, Massachusetts, who often made no effort to conceal their ignorance of, and contempt for, Americans in other parts of the country—the so-called flyover people (the people one flies over between New York and LA). During the first half of the twentieth century, however, leading Progressive thinkers like Lewis Mumford and Bernard De Voto were fascinated by America's regional diversity. The Progressive historian Frederick Jackson Turner wrote in 1932: "We have become a nation comparable to all Europe in area, with settled geographic provinces which equal great European nations. We are in this sense an empire, a federation of sections, a union of potential nations."[23]

The American regionalist movement in the arts and architecture between World War I and World War II drew eclectically on a number of traditions, including the Mexican Muralist movement initiated by the visionary Mexican statesman Jose Vasconcelos, romantic folk primitivism, Marxist "social realism," and the interest in regional planning and suburban design of two British thinkers, Patrick Geddes and Ebeneezer Howard. Some of the regionalists, like the critic Thomas

Craven, were xenophobic nativists, but the majority were political liberals. Their emphasis on modest homes for middle-class and working-
class Americans went along naturally with an emphasis on providing
ordinary citizens with public amenities like pleasant neighborhoods
and easy access to nearby parks and wilderness areas. Far from being
reactionary or nostalgic, the interest in regional folk traditions in the
arts and architecture was profoundly democratic—as was the interest
in designing the small house of the ordinary citizen instead of the Big
House of the industrial tycoon or rural landlord. Their ideal was not
the "mass" (a factory proletariat) nor the "yeoman farmer," but an educated and active middle-class citizenry at home in a humanized natural environment.

Frank Lloyd Wright, whose Prairie School was American regionalist architecture at its best, was an enthusiastic proponent of this
view. In *The Disappearing City* (1932), revised and republished in
1945 as *When Democracy Builds*, Wright named his utopia "Broadacre City"—a mosaic of small towns, small farms, single-family homes
on large parcels of land, parks, and wilderness preserves that would
completely cover the continental United States, for which he used the
eccentric term "Usonia." Something like Wright's Usonia was the
ideal of most of the New Deal regionalists—a landscape that blended
industry and agriculture, single-family homes, and small offices in a
harmonious quilt stitched together by public utilities and infrastructure using the most advanced technology of the day.

Texas had its own regionalist artistic movement in the 1920s and
1930s, centered on the *Southwest Review* and represented in the
visual arts by the "Dallas Nine" in painting, along with the Mexican-
American sculptor Oscar Medellin. The "Texas" with which they
identified was the southern extension of the Great Plains in the
Panhandle and the Hill Country. It was this region that supplied the
major regionalist artists and architects with their imagery: the Dust
Bowl farm, the stone or brick Hill Country house with a seamed metal
roof. They could find inspiration as well in the Hispanic tradition
of San Antonio and South Texas, but in their hearts these painters
and architects were children of the Great Plains. Their identification

of Texas with the Great Plains was subversive in its effect; whether they intended to do so or not, the major Texan regionalists redefined Texas as the South of the Midwest rather than the West of the Deep South.

The thread of a single life—that of David Reichard Williams (1890–1962)—connects the bohemian Dallas regionalist artistic circle with the enthusiasm for population dispersal and regional planning of Franklin and Eleanor Roosevelt, the vernacular modernism of Frank Lloyd Wright with the National Youth Administration (NYA) and Davy Crockett. Today Williams is best remembered as an architect whose followers, O'Neil Ford and his apprentices, David Lake and Ted Flato, became the most prominent Texan architects of the second half of the twentieth century. But Williams was also a government administrator and architectural photographer, a foreign development adviser, and a book illustrator. A dinner guest of Franklin and Eleanor Roosevelt, he entertained Frank Lloyd Wright at his own home in Dallas, as his father had entertained Buffalo Bill during his childhood in the Texas Panhandle.

With his friend Frank Lloyd Wright, David R. Williams shared an enthusiasm for urban and regional planning. After several years in which he was employed by the Roosevelt administration to design new communities for farm families displaced by the Depression, using innovative styles inspired by the local vernacular, Williams was appointed to the NYA, where he was chief architect and deputy administrator from 1936 to 1941. National Park buildings across the country reflect his emphasis on architecture rooted in particular regions. While at the NYA, Williams worked with Maury Maverick, the mayor of San Antonio and a prominent New Dealer whose views made him the target of intense hatred by Texan conservatives. Williams and his brilliant disciple O'Neil Ford rescued La Villita, a deteriorating slum near the Alamo, from incorporation into a downtown district and turned it into a showcase of early Mexican-Texan architecture. Once renovated, La Villita became the centerpiece of the Paseo del Rio or River Walk in San Antonio, today one of the most pleasant places in North America and a popular destination for tourists from around the world. The connection of La Villita with the Alamo was of particular importance to Williams, whose childhood idol had been Davy Crockett.[24]

The role of Williams in the NYA is less familiar today than that of one of his fellow Texans. On August 20, 1935, in the White House, President Roosevelt welcomed the state directors of the NYA. FDR, intrigued by one of them, asked him to stay behind. This administrator, who at the age of 28 was the youngest state NYA director in the country, made headlines with his idea for "roadside parks," copied throughout the United States, and his daring efforts on behalf of young black men and women, who in Texas and other segregated Southern states had their own separate NYA chapters. His name was Lyndon Johnson.[25]

In the late 1930s, public opinion turned against visionary New Deal experiments with state capitalism like the TVA and LCRA and national service programs like the NYA. Conservatives argued that FDR was trying to become a dictator like Hitler or Mussolini or Stalin—an impression that Roosevelt's 1937 scheme to pack the Supreme Court with supporters of the New Deal, like the earlier "Blue Eagle" imagery of the National Recovery Administration, inadvertently reinforced. With Pearl Harbor, military-led state capitalism eclipsed civilian state capitalism in importance. Throughout World War II and the Cold War and beyond, the Pentagon replaced agencies like the TVA as the center of American state capitalism.

The importance of World War II in the industrial transformation of the United States cannot be exaggerated. Between 1940 and 1945, nearly half of the previous total investment in all U.S. industry was in war production by the federal government. Before Pearl Harbor, the only states in which a third or more of the workforce was in the manufacturing sector were New Jersey, Pennsylvania, Ohio, Michigan, and the states of New England. Between 1950 and 1970, the share of traditional manufacturing activity in the Northeastern core declined by 3 percent and grew in the Sunbelt by a factor of 56 percent.[26]

Between the Japanese attack on Pearl Harbor on December 7, 1941, and V-J Day on August 14, 1945, the landscape and economy of Texas were transformed by military-led modernization in a revolution far more profound, and with more lasting effects, than Reconstruction or the New Deal. In addition to increasing oil and gas production, the federal government made Texas the site of factories that produced rubber from petroleum, to replace natural rubber supplies from Japanese-occupied Asia and Brazil, and also magnesium and aluminum. The government expanded and upgraded existing shipyards and created a Texan ship-building industry from nothing. The draining of the rural population into military service and factory work accelerated the mechanization of Texas agriculture, increasing its efficiency.

The Houston construction firm of Brown and Root, a longtime backer of Lyndon Johnson, grew rich from government contracts during World War II and the Cold War; in California, similar beneficiaries of military state capitalism were Kaiser Steel and Bechtel Corporation, which provided many of the members of Ronald Reagan's cabinet. (Reagan voted four times for Roosevelt for president, so his alliance with a corporate client of the Rooseveltian state was only appropriate.)

Texas Instruments, one of the largest semiconductor companies in the world, provides an illustration of the importance of military state capitalism to the growth of the contemporary tech industry. Under the name of Geophysical Services, Inc., the company first built electronics to help oil companies search for oil. During the Second World War, the company built instruments to help the navy search for enemy submarines. By 1951, when the company changed its name to Texas Instruments (TI), it had specialized in providing electronics to the U.S. military. Obtaining a license to build transistors from Bell Labs, TI built the first commercial silicon transistors and later the first integrated circuit and the first hand-held calculator. The migration of the company from the oil patch to the military-industrial sector symbolized the larger evolution of the Texas economy.

While the warfare state was the partner of Texas Instruments, H. Ross Perot's Electronic Data Systems (EDS) was in part a product of the welfare state expanded by the Great Society—the successor to the New Deal enacted in the 1960s by FDR's disciple Lyndon John-son.[27] Johnson prevailed on Congress to pass the Social Security Act of 1965, which created Medicare and Medicaid. EDS acquired a con-tract to process the flood of claims under the new Medicare program of Texas that was managed by Blue Cross/Blue Shield. Later, the ser-vices of EDS were enlisted by U.S. military and intelligence agencies. (When several of the company's technicians were stranded in Iran fol-lowing the revolution of 1979, Perot—in an act that made him a folk hero to millions of Americans—hired mercenaries to fly into Iran and rescue them.)[28]

Yet another example of state capitalism that contributed to the modernization of Texas was the space program. During the Eisen-hower administration, as Senate majority leader and chairman of the Senate's Special Committee on Space and Astronautics, Lyndon John-son played a dominant role in the creation of NASA. As Kennedy's vice-president, he mobilized public and private support for the space program, and continued to champion NASA even when public enthu-siasm for space projects began to wane in the mid-1960s. "Space was the platform from which the social revolution of the 1960s was launched," he wrote in his memoir, *The Vantage-Point*. "If we could send a man to the moon, we knew we should be able to send a poor boy to school and to provide decent medical care for the aged."[29]

Texans who oversaw congressional spending on space—Repre-sentatives Overton Brooks and Olin Teague in the House space com-mittee and Representative Albert Thomas, the chair of the House Appropriations Committee—ensured that Southwestern companies got lucrative NASA contracts. Thanks to their and Johnson's influ-ence, space operations were divided between Cape Canaveral in Florida and Houston. The first word in the first sentence transmitted from the lunar surface was the name of both a city and the charis-matic hero of San Jacinto known as the "Father of Texas"—"Houston, the *Eagle* has landed."

A generation earlier, Johnson had astounded rural Texans by descending from the sky in a helicopter at mass political rallies. For Johnson, as for Frank Lloyd Wright, who gave each exurban family in his imaginary "Broadacre City" its own helicopter in his drawings, the helicopter was a symbol of advanced technology, along with the dam and the spaceship. Although Johnson could play the cowboy as well as any Texan conservative, the pop culture imagery with which Johnson preferred to associate himself was not that of Hollywood cowboy movies and dime-store Westerns. It was the imagery of high technology and science fiction, of *Amazing Stories* and *Popular Science.*

The federal state capitalist tradition following World War II was not limited to federal investment in military bases and the space program. The Internet began its existence as a network linking scientists and engineers at universities and elsewhere who had contracts to do research for the Defense Department's Defense Advanced Research Projects Agency (DARPA). In its first incarnation, the Internet was known as DARPANET. To a degree that is seldom acknowledged, the computer revolution itself was a product of U.S. military state capitalism.

One of the most important contemporary figures in this tradition is Admiral Bobby Ray Inman, a career naval officer from Texas who became head of the National Security Administration, responsible for high-tech global surveillance, and then deputy director of the CIA (he was offered, and refused, the post of secretary of defense in the Clinton administration). Returning to Austin, where he had graduated from the University of Texas in 1950, Inman was the first chairman and chief executive officer of the Microelectronics and Computer Technology Corporation (MCC), a consortium that suffered reverses but succeeded in its larger purpose of catalyzing the growth of the tech sector in Texas by means of partnerships involving industry, government, and the academy. By the 1990s, the Silicon Hills of Austin became almost as important in the tech industry as California's Silicon Valley. Inman, appropriately enough, became Lyndon B. Johnson Centennial Professor at the LBJ School of Public Affairs in Austin. He was the second to hold the Johnson chair; the first had been Johnson's protégé and the first black woman to serve in the U.S. House of Representatives from Texas, Barbara Jordan.[30]

Jordan A. Schwarz, whose book *The New Dealers* (1993) is the best account of the subject, summarizes the accomplishments of the Texan modernists in Texas and the rest of the country:

For developing regions, markets and credit, the New Dealers were a godsend. That sterling trio of Texans Sam Rayburn, Lyndon Johnson and Wright Patman appreciated what Washington could do for Texas—and Oregon and Mississippi—as well as its political rewards. State capitalism was not an oxymoron for them; it boded abundance and creature comforts for their constituents. They became evangelists of state capitalism. They used the credit revolution to manufacture cheap power that brought opportunistic corporate capital and growth to the South and West. It would take decades to overcome Southern poverty and Western sparseness of population before growth would become a questionable addiction in parts of Florida and California, but by 1980 a national New Deal mentality had generated the sunbelt.

Schwarz concludes: "Most of all, the New Deal built the modern middle class."[31] The visionary Texans who helped to create the modern American middle class were almost all members of the middle class themselves. The argument that the politics of class is alien to America is not borne out by the history of Texas. The struggle between the Texan modernists and the Texan traditionalists was largely a class war within a highly homogeneous Southern white Protestant population. There were a few conservatives from humble backgrounds, like John Nance Garner and Coke Stevenson, and a small number of well-bred Texan modernists, like Colonel House. But most of the leaders of the Texan right, like both Bushes, were born into affluent if not rich families. Jesse Jones, the most important conservative Texan in the New Deal years, was born to a rich planter in Tennessee whose ten-room brick house was described as "the finest outside of Nashville."[32] Allen Shivers, the reactionary red-baiting and racist governor during the 1950s, was described by a historian in 1979 as "a landed aristocrat from the valley [South Texas]."[33] The father of another "landed aristocrat from the valley," Lloyd Bentsen, owned a farming and ranching empire in South Texas and controlled eight banks. James Baker of Baker & Botts was heir to a Houston dynasty.

By contrast, the Texan modernists typically came from middle-class, working-class, or even poor families. Sam Rayburn came from a poor farm family, picked cotton as a child, and rode a horse six miles each day to high school. Lyndon Johnson grew up in a poor region in a family that had fallen on hard times, and Ralph Yarborough came from a middle-class family in a small East Texas town. When a lobbyist for a major oil company attended a victory party that celebrated Yarborough's election to the U.S. Senate in 1956, he was puzzled, reporting, "No big shots there, just people."[34] Ross Perot was the son of a horse trader and cotton broker in Texarkana, and Bobby Ray Inman, another product of the small-town middle-class born in Rhonesboro, Texas, attended the public schools of Austin rather than an elite private academy. Homer Rainey and John Connally, the liberal modernist and the conservative modernist, came from similar small-town backgrounds. Almost all were Baptists, Methodists, or members of other low-church Protestant denominations. They were not elite liberals, motivated by noblesse oblige, for whom politics is a form of philanthropy. When rural electrification permitted kerosene lamps to be replaced by light switches, it was their families and their neighbors who benefited. And when Americans were drafted to fight in World War II and the Cold War, it was their brothers, sons, cousins, and nephews who fought and sometimes died. They were worthy heirs of Philip Dru.

FOUR

Southernomics

The influence of enlightened Texan modernism on American society peaked in 1964 and 1965, when President Lyndon Johnson, after
being elected by a landslide majority, presided over the enactment of
some of the most important legislation in U.S. history. Not only did
Johnson complete the unfinished New Deal by creating the Medicare
and Medicaid programs, but he also pushed through the Civil Rights
Act and the Voting Rights Act, which finally abolished formal racism
in the United States a century after the Civil War. Franklin Roosevelt,
the political mentor who had promoted Johnson's career, would have
been impressed and proud.

Not until 2000, thirty-six years later, did another Republican candidate lose the popular vote on the scale on which Barry Goldwater
lost to Lyndon Johnson. The votes for Al Gore and Ralph Nader, added
together, produced the greatest popular-vote majority for the center-
left since 1964. But as a result of Ralph Nader's third-party candidacy,
rural over-representation in the electoral college, and the intervention
of the conservative majority on the Supreme Court, George W. Bush,
rejected by most American voters, became president of the United
States.

During the 2000 presidential campaign, many Americans believed
that Bush's slogan of "compassionate conservatism" and the appoint-
ment of Colin Powell, a self-described "Rockefeller Republican," as
secretary of state signaled a shift by the second President Bush toward
the political center. Instead, in his first two years in office Bush was
the most rigidly dogmatic conservative ideologue in the White House

since before the Great Depression. His uncompromising conservatism cost the Republicans the Senate by driving the moderate Republican senator from Vermont, Jim Jeffords, to become an independent. And the radical conservatism of his foreign policy, manifested in a spree of unilateral cancelations of treaties by the United States and a reflexive support of the brutal Israeli government of Ariel Sharon in the volatile Middle East, by the spring of 2002 had alienated almost all of America's European and Middle Eastern allies, squandering the sympathy that other nations had felt for the United States after the terrorist attacks of September 11, 2001.

What distinguished Bush from his father and Reagan was not his free-market economic agenda. After all, conservatives of various persuasions, along with libertarians who rejected conservative social views, supported the large tax cut enacted by Congress in 2001, as well as the Bush administration's support for the partial privatization of Social Security and school choice. But these familiar issues of the conservative/libertarian right were not what gave the Bush brand of conservatism its unique flavor. Although Bush's ancestors were Northeastern, the culture that shaped him was made in Texas—a culture that combines Protestant fundamentalism and Southern militarism with an approach to economics that favors primitive commodity capitalist enterprises like cotton and oil production over high-tech manufacturing and scientific R&D. For generations, this synthesis has retarded the social and economic progress of Texas. Now, thanks to rural over-representation in the electoral college, the alliance of the country church and the country club had captured Washington, D.C.

George W. Bush was not the first Texan to be elected president, nor the first conservative to be elected president. But he was the first Texan conservative to be elected president.

The second Bush administration, from its first days in office, was far more consistently right-wing than the administrations of Ronald Reagan and George H. W. Bush had been. Although Reagan had been quite conservative, his presidential coalition had been a broad one, diluting the influence of Southern conservatives by uniting them with old-fashioned Northern moderate Republicans; socially conservative, economically populist working-class Reagan Democrats in the industrial states; socially liberal libertarians; and centrist "neoconservatives" who were disenchanted with the 1960s left but suspicious of the anti-government ideology of the "Old Right." His successor, the first President Bush, was a transitional figure who blended the hard-edged conservatism of the Sunbelt with the more moderate approach of the old Northeastern patriciate and its allies in corporate boardrooms in the South and West.

By the time George W. Bush ran for president in 2000, the Southernization of the Republican Party was complete. The Southern right dominated a party that was shrinking as it lost members in other parts of the country to Democrats and independent candidates. The party of Lincoln had become the party of Jefferson Davis.

The electoral map in 2000 told the story. The Republican Party was the party of the South and the Prairie/Mountain West. The size of the latter gave a misleading sense of the importance of the interior West, because the demographic center of the GOP was the much more densely populated South.

The electoral map told another story in 2000. The Republicans had become the party of the countryside and small towns, in a predominantly urban and suburban America. George Bush won 80 percent of the counties in the United States, Al Gore only 20 percent. In addition to being the rural party, the Republicans were also the white party, in a nation in which the numbers of white Americans was shrinking relative to those of black, Latino, Asian, and mixed-race Americans. About 95 percent of the vote for Bush came from whites, who made up 75 percent of the national population. Among white ethnic groups, only Jews strongly preferred Gore. Although Bush received the greatest support from white voters with incomes higher than $100,000, whites at all socioeconomic levels—including poor whites with incomes under $15,000—gave Bush a slight majority of their votes. Bush also won a slight majority of white women (49–48). The "gender gap" existed only because non-white women preferred the Democratic Party. During the Republican Convention, party leaders paraded blacks and Latinos across the stage in order to create an illusion of diversity. Although blacks made up only 4 percent of the Republican delegates, they made up 21 percent of the speakers in the opening sessions; Latinos accounted for 3 percent of the delegates and 12 percent of the speakers. The performances of black rap singers and black gospel singers before an overwhelmingly white delegate audience, almost half of whom were worth at least $500,000, had an unintended resemblance to a minstrel show.[1] Notwithstanding the Republican Party's outreach efforts, in November 2000 Gore got 90 percent of the black vote, 62 percent of the Latino vote, and 55 percent of the Asian-American vote. Ninety-five percent of black Texans and more than 60 percent of Latino Texans voted against their governor in the presidential race.

And the Republicans were the religious party, doing the best among the most devout members of all denominations—Protestant, Catholic, and Jewish—while doing poorly among Americans whose religious affiliation was nominal and vestigial, as well as among the growing number of completely secular Americans.

The rural, the religious, and the white—this was the social base of George W. Bush's Southern-based Republican Party. Far smaller than the Reagan coalition, this Southern party and its Western wing would have won only the House of Representatives in the 2000 election if not for rural over-representation. In the form of the malapportioned Senate, which exaggerates the importance of the thinly populated interior West by assigning each state two senators, rural over-representation gave the Republicans a precarious majority in the 2000 election. And rural over-representation, in the form of the electoral college, which similarly exaggerates the weight of small-population states, permitted George W. Bush to be elected president—even though Al Gore won the popular vote, and even though the votes for Al Gore and Ralph Nader, combined, created the largest popular-vote landslide for the center-left since 1964. The result of the bitterly contested election of 2000 was as though Lyndon Johnson had trounced Barry Goldwater—who had nevertheless gone on to win the presidency, as a result of the archaic electoral college.

George W. Bush is the first Southern conservative to be elected president of the United States since James Knox Polk in 1844. In the intervening generations, there have been Southern presidents and there have been conservative presidents. But the Southern presidents have not been conservative, and the conservative presidents have not been Southern.

There have been other Southern presidents since Appomattox: Wilson (born and raised in the South), Truman (a native of the Southern part of the Midwest), Johnson, Carter, and Clinton. But the Southern presidents of the twentieth century, from Wilson to Clinton, were all progressives or liberals, by the standards of the South if not always of the nation. George W. Bush, born in New Haven, Connecticut, but reared in the reactionary culture of Anglo-Southern West Texas, is different in kind. Bush's political ancestors are not the Southern presidents of the twentieth century, but reactionary Southern senators and representatives who dominated the Democratic Party from the early nineteenth century until the New Deal, and who took over the Republican Party in the 1990s.

While George W. Bush is far more conservative than previous Southern presidents, he is also far more Southern than previous conservative presidents. In the early twentieth century, conservative Republican presidents like Taft, Hoover, and Coolidge represented the right wing of the Lincoln Republican tradition. The political and cultural values of the Northern Republican base in Greater New England—New England proper, the Midwest, and the Pacific Northwest—have always been antithetical to those of the Southern elite. The Northern Republicans were protectionists, not free-traders like the Southerners; they were as committed to civilian values as Southerners traditionally have been committed to the martial ethic; in foreign policy, they preferred an isolationist or minimalist policy to the expansive, militaristic, unilateral policy preferred by generations of Southern hawks. The conservative heirs of Lincoln and McKinley in the North and the conservative heirs of Jefferson Davis in the South have sought to conserve incompatible traditions. The Northern right and the Southern right may have had common enemies—for example, in organized labor—but on the most basic questions about the nature and fate of the United States they have disagreed with each other. Indeed, they fought a civil war.

George W. Bush's brand of conservatism is also far more Southern in character than that of recent Republican presidents like Richard Nixon, Ronald Reagan, and his own father. While Nixon used a "Southern strategy" to win over white Southern conservative Democrats to the Republican Party, his GOP was still primarily a party of the Midwest, the Northeast, and the West Coast. Reagan, more of a conservative ideologue than Nixon and Eisenhower, led a large and fractious coalition in which Southern conservatives were only one element, along with moderate business-class Republicans, Northern working-class Catholic "Reagan Democrats," and Jewish Cold War liberals. Under the first George Bush in the White House, the Reagan coalition shrank, losing many of its moderate voters, and forcing the elder Bush, a Northeastern moderate by instinct, to engage in clumsy attempts to appease the Southern right. Far more homogeneous than the Reagan coalition of the 1980s, the Republican Party of George W. Bush consists chiefly of former white Southern Democrats, allied with a small but influential group of Jewish reactionaries who compose a shrunken relic of the once-flourishing Democratic neoconservative movement of the 1970s and 1980s. The base of the conservative movement had shrunk to white Southern conservatives and Jewish-American supporters of Israel's right wing by the beginning of the twenty-first century.

George W. Bush, then, is the representative of the Southern conservative oligarchy—a regional elite that has never, since the days of the Jeffersonian and Jacksonian presidential "dynasties," dominated the White House and the executive branch the way it did beginning in January 2001.

The second Bush administration represented more than the grafting of traditional Texan conservatism on the federal government. It was also the culmination of seventy years of a counter-revolution against the New Deal, in both domestic policy and foreign policy. In the 1950s and 1960s, moderate Republicans like Dwight Eisenhower, Richard Nixon, and Nelson Rockefeller accepted the Rooseveltian welfare state and Rooseveltian liberal internationalism. But from the 1930s on, much of the Southern elite had angrily rejected the reforms of Franklin Roosevelt and his successors like Truman and Johnson. Under names like the "Jeffersonian Democrats" and the "Texas Regulars," they conspired repeatedly to deny Roosevelt reelection. In 1948, many of them followed Strom Thurmond out of the Democratic Party into the segregationist States' Rights Party. By the 1990s, most conservative white Southern Democrats had followed Thurmond into the Republican Party, enabling it to gain control of both houses of Congress in 1994 and 2002 and of the White House in 2000. With leaders like the Texans George W. Bush, Tom DeLay, Phil Gramm, and Dick Armey, contemporary American conservatism speaks not only with a Southern accent but with a Texan drawl.

Southern opposition to the policies of FDR and his allies long antedated the Civil Rights Revolution of the 1950s and 1960s. Southern conservatives had never accepted the terms of the mid-twentieth-century social contract known as the New Deal. In the realm of political economy, these Southern reactionaries preferred the Old Deal that had existed between the end of Reconstruction and the Great Depression: a laissez-faire economy with minimal federal regulation. Instead of being protected by a government safety net, these anti–New Deal conservatives have always believed that the poor should rely, as they had done before 1932, chiefly on religious charity and private philanthropy.

In most of the country in the second half of the twentieth century, not to mention other advanced industrial democracies, such notions were eccentric. But generations of Southerners who belonged to the social and political elite were raised to believe that Franklin Roosevelt, like Abraham Lincoln, had been a usurper and a tyrant. Dick Armey, a Republican representative from Dallas, spoke for this faction when, in his 1995 book *The Freedom Revolution,* he compared Franklin Roosevelt to Stalin and Mao. At the time that he made this observation, Armey was the third most important leader in the House of Representatives, a body once dominated by Sam Rayburn, Wright Patman, the young Lyndon Johnson, and other Texan reformers. Nothing could better symbolize the success of the Southern counter-revolution against the New Deal.

Beginning in the 1970s, the Southern counter-revolutionaries began to win important victories in national politics—ironically, by exploiting one of the proudest achievements of the New Deal, the industrialization of the agrarian periphery. The New Deal Democrats who successfully modernized the South and the West inadvertently gave Southern and Western conservatives an advantage in both politics and political economy in the final quarter of the twentieth century. By creating an industrial infrastructure throughout the country, the New Dealers eliminated a major disadvantage of the South and the West. This they had intended to do. But they also gave the low-tax, low-wage states of the South and the West an advantage in competing with the old industrial Northeast for footloose industries.

The progressive New Deal modernists had sought to nationalize American society as well as the American economy—to level the playing field in disputes between capital and labor, as well as in sectional competition for industry and investment. But this aspect of the New Deal economic project was never realized. Franklin Roosevelt's failed campaign to purge the Southern Democrats of conservatives in the congressional elections of 1938 backfired, creating a "conservative coalition" of Southern Democrats and Republicans that dominated Congress until the 1970s. The conservative coalition passed New Deal measures that benefited business in the South and the West— and killed reforms that would have helped ordinary workers in the periphery. For example, Southern Democrats in Congress exempted agricultural and domestic workers—two categories that included most black Americans in the South—from Social Security laws. In the 1940s, Lyndon Johnson's partner Herman Brown worked with the Texas legislature to pass anti-union legislation. Brown and Root liked government subsidies for rural electrification, but not government legislation on behalf of organized labor.

Following World War II, many companies in the Northeast and

Midwest transferred their factories and sometimes their headquarters to the South and West, to take advantage of low wages and low taxes. Two scholars write that "industrial location choices are governed to a lesser extent than in the past by access to markets, labor transportation and raw materials. While these traditional locational determinants exert an important influence, the list of important locational determinants has been expanded to include state and local taxes, education, business climate, labor skills and state and local physical infrastructure. In fact, at the high technology end of the industrial spectrum, these non-traditional location factors tend to dominate the location choices."[2] Notice that state and local taxes come first on the list.

The low-tax states attracted business from other parts of the world, as well as from other parts of the United States. Beginning in the 1970s, foreign direct investment grew dramatically in the South and the West, as car manufacturers based in Germany and Japan opened up factories in places like Tennessee and Alabama to take advantage of the anti-union, low-wage "business climate." In 1985, Jared Hazelton, whose Texas Research League was funded by the business community, bragged: "We are a low-tax, low-service state."[3]

The decentralists of the New Deal wanted industries to disperse throughout the country—but not in order to take advantage of anti-labor laws and a low level of spending on government services in states dominated by reactionary conservatives. Between the 1930s and the 1970s, "modern Republicans" like Eisenhower and Nixon as well as Rooseveltian Democrats like Truman, Kennedy, and Johnson had tried to level the playing field among the states in public spending as well as in infrastructure. Their preferred method was revenue sharing—using the federal government to raise taxes nationwide, and then distributing them more or less on the basis of population. Because high-income taxpayers tend to be concentrated in a few neighborhoods in a few metro areas in a few states, revenue sharing is a disguised form of redistribution from the rich to the rest both within and between states. New Deal politicians in the South and West could sometimes be brutally frank about the fact that they were taxing Northeastern millionaires to pay for local projects. In the 1930s, U.S. Representative Lyndon Johnson told one Texan businessman: "What are you worried about? It's not coming out of your pocket. Any money that's spent here on New Deal projects, the East is paying for. We don't pay any taxes in Texas. . . . They're paying for our projects."[4] Even if states and localities misused federal revenue-sharing grants, the result tended to be more equitable; at least some of the money would "trickle down" to the needy, and thanks to revenue sharing there was more money in most states than there would have been otherwise.

Federal revenue sharing makes a more progressive tax system possible. In a federal system, it is much easier for the central government than for state or provincial governments to impose progressive taxes on income (and, in theory, on consumption and wealth). Individuals may move from one federal subunit to another to escape income taxes—but hardly anyone, no matter how rich, will leave the country and become a "tax expatriate." The tendency of income taxes to frighten away residents and corporations explains why so many states, even relatively progressive ones, are forced to rely on regressive taxes like property taxes, sales taxes, and user fees that consume a greater proportion of the incomes of the poor and working class than of the affluent. Real estate cannot be moved among jurisdictions, and the use of sales taxes and user fees hides the true amount of taxation from state residents.

Among the champions of federal revenue sharing were Melvin Laird, a Republican from progressive Wisconsin, who introduced legislation in 1958, and Walter Heller, the chairman of the Council of Economic Advisors to the Kennedy and Johnson administrations. In 1972, with the support of the Nixon administration, Congress enacted a General Revenue Sharing (GRS) program, which provided federal funds with few strings attached to states until 1981 and to local governments until 1986. The federal share of state and local revenues rose to one-quarter at its peak during the Johnson and Nixon years. Unfortunately, General Revenue Sharing was abolished in 1986 as part of efforts to reduce the federal deficit created by the Reagan tax cuts.[5] The program had never been popular either with conservative proponents of limited government or with liberals who preferred narrow categorical grants or broad block grants aimed at particularly constituencies like the urban poor or limited to certain purposes like public health. An indirect effect of the abolition of general revenue sharing was to increase the differences in spending by state and local governments between the low-tax states of the periphery and the high-tax states of the industrial Northeast—helping the former lure enterprises and industries from the latter.

Ironically, then, conservatives benefited from the fact that the New Deal succeeded in leveling the industrial playing field nationwide, while failing to reduce or eliminate the regional disparities in labor laws, taxation, and public spending that allowed peripheral states to attract business. The New Deal modernists built an infrastructure for the South and West that traditional conservatives inherited and used for their own illiberal purposes.

The Southern right and its political and intellectual allies, beginning in the 1970s, also triumphed in the debate over international trade. A commitment to international economic integration was shared by most of the American politicians and civil servants who helped to create a new international economic order after 1945. The preference of the Southern commodity-exporting sector for a free-trade regime that guaranteed access to foreign markets for agricultural goods and raw materials influenced Southern internationalists like FDR's secretary of state, Cordell Hull, who led the campaign to reduce or eliminate tariffs worldwide.

Following World War II, the challenge in most of the world, outside of Europe and Japan, was not to revive existing industries but to industrialize agrarian countries, most of them former colonies of one or another European empire. Many American statesmen and intellectuals believed that the success of New Deal-style state capitalism in modernizing the rural South and West in the United States had lessons for developing countries in Latin America, Africa, Asia, and the Middle East. In 1944, David Lilienthal, the director of the TVA, published a book entitled *TVA: Democracy on the March*, in which he argued for the worldwide relevance of the TVA model as an alternative to laissez-faire capitalism and bureaucratic socialism. Adolf Berle promoted a

TVA in the Sao Francisco Valley of Brazil, while Harry Truman spoke of a TVA on the Yangtze River in China and Lyndon Johnson of a TVA in the Mekong River Delta. The Truman administration's Point Four program was designed to help poor countries catch up by a mix of public investment and private enterprise like that of the New Deal.[6]

In much of the developing world, ethnic warfare and government corruption retarded economic progress of any kind. American enthusiasm for foreign TVA-style capitalism was a casualty of growing conservatism in American politics after the 1960s.

Slow growth and runaway inflation in the 1970s were blamed by free-market conservatives and libertarians on the combination of Keynesian management of the economy and large welfare states that had become the norm in North America and Western Europe following World War II. Milton Friedman and other free-market fundamentalists became global celebrities, and a cult of Adam Smith was established on both sides of the Atlantic. The arguments of the free-market theorists were far from convincing, but their message was disseminated by think tanks funded by Wall Street tycoons. In the South, where the New Deal had made only a dent, the free-market revival merely confirmed the regional preference for free trade, laissez-faire, and minimal government regulation of employers and property owners.

By the 1980s and 1990s, the new free-market consensus, under the name of "neoliberalism," became accepted by center-left as well as the center-right in both the United States and Britain (it was less influential in continental Europe and East Asia). There was little for free-market enthusiasts to do with respect to trade and capital flows among the industrial democracies, which had already been liberalized between the 1940s and the 1970s. The greatest break with the Rooseveltian consensus, therefore, took place in policies toward the developing economies. By the 1980s, nobody in Washington spoke of exporting the TVA model to Africa or South Asia anymore. The new model was export-oriented manufacturing. According to the neoliberal consensus, entire continents could develop the way that a few small East Asian countries like South Korea and Taiwan had done—by becoming low-wage manufacturing platforms for multinational corporations, making and selling products to affluent consumers in the United States and other rich nations. The fact that the successful export-oriented countries had protected their own markets while taking advantage of unimpeded access to America's consumer market was seldom mentioned by the theorists who held that global free trade would quickly and painlessly produce global modernization.

The export-oriented model of development did not necessarily require capital mobility. Even so, acting on behalf of the Wall Street investment community from which he came, the Clinton administration's secretary of the treasury, Robert Rubin, pressured developing countries into liberalizing their capital markets. If the hydroelectric plant was the symbol of New Deal-style development, the new national stock exchange joined the maquiladora or technology park as a symbol of economic development. The money of North American and Western European investors flooded into enterprises in Eastern Europe, Russia, and much of Asia—only to flow out again when investors were spooked, leaving entire economies to collapse like deflating balloons. In the mid-1990s, the Asian financial crisis, caused by a flight of nervous Western capital, created conditions through much of Asia comparable to those in the Great Depression. China and Malaysia, which had refused to follow the advice of American economists and policymakers to liberalize their capital markets, were spared.

Just as damaging was the role of the International Monetary Fund (IMF) during the years of the post-Rooseveltian free-market revival. The IMF had been intended by its designers in the 1940s to help out the advanced industrial countries during financial crises. Instead, by the late twentieth century it had become an enforcer for private investors in the developing world. Often it advised already desperate countries to adopt drastic and unpopular austerity plans in return for loans.

Nothing could have been further from the Rooseveltian strategy of development by means of state-capitalist infrastructure projects and ample public credit than the neoliberal formula of export-processing sweatshops, Potemkin village stock exchanges, and national austerity plans imposed by foreign lenders. If Texas and other Southern and Western states had tried to catch up with the industrial Northeast by following such a strategy, they would be largely rural societies to this day. But of course, a rural agrarian South was what many opponents of the Rooseveltians in the Southern ruling class wanted all along.

The rehabilitation of free-market conservatism in the late-twentieth-century United States influenced how the American elite thought about international trade as well as international development. From the end of World War II until the 1970s, global economic liberalization won the support of most American manufacturers and most of organized labor, for two major reasons. The first was the devastation by war of the industries of Europe and East Asia, which eliminated much foreign competition for American manufacturers; the second was the fact that most international trade was among developed nations with comparable wages and living standards. By the 1970s, the recovery of Europe and East Asia had eliminated America's temporary monopoly on manufactured exports, while the transfer of manufacturing from the United States to low-wage countries had altered the second condition. In response, from the 1970s on, organized labor, and purely national U.S. businesses, became increasingly protectionist. Support for global free trade was found chiefly in its traditional home—the commodity-exporting states of the South and the West—as well as among multinational corporations and their American investors. Free trade, then, meant something different in the 1945–1973 period than it did in the 1973–2000 period. Between 1945 and 1973, the emphasis of U.S. trade policy was on increasing intra-industry trade among similar countries; Germany and the United States, for example, both made cars and bought cars from one another. After 1973, the subject of the debate changed to economic integration between rich countries and poor countries with radically different income levels, labor and environmental standards, and political systems. Opponents of the integration of the economies of rich and poor countries argued that the result would be the transfer not only of manufacturing but of service-sector jobs to the poor countries, by companies seeking to take advantage of low wage rates and, in some cases, governments hostile to worker rights and indifferent to the environment. The proponents of trade liberalization beyond the circle of developed nations argued that both affluent and poor countries would derive enormous benefits from the merger of their economies.

The debate over the North American Free Trade Area (NAFTA) dramatized these issues. The division within the United States over NAFTA was not partisan, but geographic and economic. Opposition was concentrated in the industrial states of the Northeast and Midwest, while support was strongest in the commodity-sector states of the South and West. Affluent Americans, many of whom hoped that foreign investments would fatten their retirement accounts, generally supported trade liberalization, while working-class Americans, afraid that they would lose their jobs to competing factories or businesses in Mexico, tended to oppose NAFTA.

After presidential candidate Ross Perot debated Vice-President Al Gore on national television in 1992, the conventional wisdom held that Gore had won the debate and that Perot had been exposed as an economic illiterate. Perot's prediction of a "giant sucking sound" coming from Mexico was widely derided by commentators who claimed that Perot had predicted mass unemployment following the passage of NAFTA. In fact, Perot and other opponents of NAFTA warned that passage of the treaty would be followed by a wave of plant relocations from the United States to Mexico by U.S. corporations seeking to take advantage of the poverty of Mexican workers. Proponents of NAFTA like Gore and Clinton and most conservative and libertarian Republicans claimed that a free-trade zone between the United States and Mexico would provide jobs for Americans making and selling manufactured goods to Mexican consumers. Perot and other skeptics predicted that instead Mexican workers too poor to afford the products that they made would work for U.S.-based multinationals, making products that would then be shipped north to American consumers.[7]

A decade later, U.S. government data make it clear that, the conventional wisdom notwithstanding, Perot was right. According to one economist:

US/Mexico trade patterns are now fundamentally different from what they were before Nafta and from what supporters assume has remained unchanged. For example, the US had large net sales of computers and components . . . to Mexico *before* Nafta but had net payments to Mexico of -\$3.8 billion for these high-tech goods in 2000. The large *US net export losses to Mexico since Nafta are concentrated in autos, machinery, electronics, apparel and furniture. US net export gains are largely in agribusiness and bulk commodities such as cereals and organic chemicals.* Even the few manufactured goods with net export gains are concentrated in packing and boxes of plastic, paper and styrene largely destined briefly "in bond" to Mexico's Maquiladoras and quickly back to US consumers. (emphasis in the original)[8]

The majority of "trade" between the United States and Mexico is nothing more than the shipment of parts to Mexican maquiladoras, where low-wage workers assemble them and ship them to U.S. consumers. To quote the same authority again: "In the 12 months to March 2001, producers in Mexico exported 969,700 cars to the US alone while firms producing in the US exported only 486,800 cars to the entire world including Mexico."[9] The United Auto Workers union members who supported Ross Perot in 1992 turn out to have been right in fearing that their employers were eager to shut down American factories and replace them with new assembly plants south of the Rio Grande.

The proponents of NAFTA who claimed that it would increase the exports of manufactured goods from the United States to Mexico and scoffed at predictions that NAFTA would encourage the relocation of American-owned factories from the high-wage United States to low-wage Mexico, have been refuted by events. Another argument made by NAFTA proponents in the 1990s has also been refuted. Many claimed that the integration of the U.S. and Mexican economies would make the United States more competitive in world markets. If the NAFTA parties—the United States, Mexico, and Canada—are treated as a single economic entity, North America, then between the enactment of NAFTA in 1993 and 2000, North American exports declined in the field of vehicles, computers/mechanicals, and electric machinery, while North America had a deficit in manufactured goods from cars to computers with other industrialized regions—chiefly East Asia. According to the U.S. government, with the exception of optical goods and photographic goods, the major exports of the U.S.-Mexican-Canadian North American bloc to the rest of the world were all agricultural commodities or raw materials, including paper pulp, "meat and edible offal," chemicals, oil seeds, fertilizers, starches, and the like.[10]

From the eighteenth century on, the Southern plantation oligarchy was content for the United States (or a separate Southern confederacy) to specialize in exporting agricultural goods and raw materials to more industrial nations, importing manufactured goods in return. Thanks to the predominance in national politics of the South and Southwest since the 1970s, what was once the foreign economic strategy of the Confederate States of America has become the trade policy of the United States as a whole.

While manufacturing jobs and some service-sector jobs can be transferred to foreign countries to take advantage of low wages, many service-sector jobs ranging from construction to nursing necessarily are performed within the United States. For this dilemma, the economic strategists of the Southern right and their allies have an answer: if American jobs cannot be transferred to poor foreign workers abroad, bring the poor foreign workers to the American jobs.

Early in his administration, George W. Bush announced his support for an amnesty program for the several million illegal immigrants in the United States. President Vicente Fox of Mexico, the first president from the conservative, pro-business PAN Party, favored an even more radical policy of open borders for labor. Oligarchic elites on both sides of the Rio Grande shared an interest in promoting northward migration by the Mexican poor. Mexico would be relieved of the responsibility of providing for them, while the immigrants would depress wages in the United States and weaken organized labor—all to the benefit of American employers, who already enjoy a buyer's market in cheap labor, thanks to high levels of unskilled immigration since the 1970s. The idea of an amnesty and a regularized guest-worker program was favored on the left by Latino activists, who wish to increase the Latino population, and thus their own sociopolitical base, at the expense of working-class Latinos if necessary. This logic explains the unusual alliance between U.S. business elites and ethnic organizations like La Raza Unida on this issue. Democrats, seeking to capitalize on their advantage among Latino voters, supported the idea of an amnesty. The chief opposition came from nativist social conservatives.

Enter Phil Gramm, the senior U.S. senator from Texas, a Georgia native and conservative Democrat who became a high-profile convert to the Republican Party. In 2000, the House Judiciary Committee approved the "Agricultural Opportunities Act," the first large agricultural guest-worker program since the Bracero program, which brought 4 to 5 million Mexican farmworkers to United States, was eliminated in 1964. Gramm was ambitious. He wanted Mexican guest-workers to be used not only in agriculture, but construction, restaurants, hotels, landscaping, and other industries which white Southerners consider undignified and fit only for non-white laborers, native or foreign.

When Latino political advocacy organizations wanted to help guest-workers become naturalized U.S. citizens, the senior U.S. senator from Texas announced that any guest-worker program that made it easier for Mexican farm-workers to obtain U.S. citizenship would pass "over my cold, dead political body." Under the old Bracero program, many immigrant workers were cheated by employers who withheld their wages; the workers possessed no rights under U.S. labor laws or civil liberties laws. Gramm's version of a new Bracero program would have required the guest workers to return to their home countries each year to apply for reentry—a provision that might allow employers to punish any workers who complained by not renewing their contracts.[11] According to the historian Cindy Hahamovitch, the actual purpose of the original Bracero program between the 1940s and the 1960s was not economic, but political—to discourage wage increases and unionization following the Great Depression.[12] A modern Bracero program would have similar effects.

Even if a new Bracero program were enacted, it is far from clear that growers and businesses in Texas and the American Southwest would obey the law. During the Eisenhower era, the Texas historian Frank Goodwyn explained why Texas ranchers undermined the original Bracero program: "The wetback, having no legal status, is more completely within the farmer's little autonomous principality. He costs almost nothing and can be kept as long as the farmer sees fit. Therefore, he can be made to take the place formerly occupied by serfs and slaves, whereas the contract laborer cannot."[13] For the contemporary Southwestern heirs of the Southern planters, if slavery is not permitted then employing foreign workers without civil rights—"coolies"—is the second best solution. They cannot vote, and if they make trouble they can be denied their deferred wages and perhaps deported.

In the aftermath of September 11, public alarm about the inadequacy of the Immigration and Naturalization Service (INS) and anxiety about the ease with which hostile foreigners had infiltrated the United States dimmed the prospects for both mass amnesties of illegal immigrants and guest-worker programs of the kind favored by the Texan spokesmen for Southwestern agribusiness. But the conviction of conservatives that economic progress can be equated with a larger workforce with lower wages and fewer rights and benefits was unlikely to die. It was, after all, far older than the United States itself, rooted as it was in the late-medieval plantation economies that Britain, Spain, and other European empires established in the Americas in the 1500s and 1600s.

What might be called "Southernomics" is based, like pre-industrial agrarian economics, on extensive development, not intensive development. Growth results from the employment of the same primitive, wasteful techniques—"the way my Daddy and Grand-daddy did it"—on additional resources, which may be the human resource of labor or natural resources like land. The traditional attitude toward resources of all too many Texans was expressed by a unanimous resolution adopted in 1898 by a meeting of cattlemen in West Texas: "*Resolved*, that none of us know, or care to know, anything about grasses, native or otherwise, outside the fact that at present there are lots of them, the best on record, and we are after getting the most out of them while they last."[14]

The free-market law of supply and demand, according to which reductions in the supply of land and labor should stimulate an increase in the demand for efficient technology, can be indefinitely evaded, according to Southernomics, by the addition of more land or the enlargement of the workforce by immigration or the expatriation of industries to new countries. Running out of oil and gas? Don't make car engines more efficient, or power vehicles with hydrogen or electric batteries; drill in wildlife preserves and conquer oil-producing countries in the Middle East, installing pro-American puppet regimes. Is there a tight labor market? Don't invest in a machine that permits one worker to do the work of three; hire illegal aliens, while lobbying the government for guest-worker programs and increased immigration quotas. The pre-modern mind can conceive of economic expansion only in terms of applying traditional techniques to more resources. The idea of using innovative machinery or more efficient organizational techniques to produce more with the same amount of land, labor, or raw materials—or even with smaller amounts—is alien to this archaic mentality.

But the assumption that there are certain industries, like agriculture, that are doomed by their very nature to use only labor-intensive, low-technology methods, is a myth. Agribusiness responds to market incentives like any other capitalist enterprise. If wages go up, as a result of minimum wage laws, unionization, or low levels of immigration, agribusiness will respond by investing in more productive technology and adopting innovative techniques to enable fewer workers to harvest more.

History confirms the thesis that high wages promote the adoption of more productive technology by agribusiness. In the nineteenth-century United States, Northern agriculture was mechanized generations earlier than Southern agriculture because the high wages of farm-workers in the labor-scarce North gave farmers an incentive to invest in labor-saving machinery like the McCormick Reaper and, later, gasoline-powered tractors and combines. Today, thanks to its low levels of immigration, Europe is far ahead of the United States in the development of robotic harvesting techniques, which all but eliminate the need for manual labor. Japan leads the world in hydroponic agriculture, which minimizes the need for farm labor in that high-wage, low-immigrant society. In Australia, where immigration is low, farmers devised a labor-saving method called "dried-on-the-vine" (DOV) harvesting, which is just as productive but reduces labor demand at harvest time by 85 percent.[15] By contrast, in today's California, where legal and illegal immigration from Mexico has created a buyer's market in unskilled labor, the same crop is harvested using labor-intensive rather than technology-intensive methods. Every year in twenty-first-century California, 40,000 to 50,000 unskilled workers harvest grapes in Central Valley, cutting each bunch of grapes by hand. Indeed, in the United States as a whole, after the Bracero program was ended in 1964, mechanization allowed Southwestern agribusiness to increase production while paying fewer workers more money. The harvesting of tomatoes in California quadrupled and real prices fell.[16] Inevitably, the high levels of unskilled immigration that began rising in the 1970s led to a decrease in the real wages of farm workers from $6.89 per hour in 1989 to $6.18 an hour in 1998.[17]

Texas itself provides a lesson in the mechanization of agriculture. Cotton harvesting was a notoriously labor-intensive activity. During the 1940s, however, researchers at Texas Agricultural and Mechanical College (A&M) learned how to mechanize cotton picking. The result was the transformation of cotton agriculture from a primitive, labor-intensive activity to a capital-intensive, heavily mechanized enterprise.[18]

Two historians of the world economy make the point that agricultural and mining economies, no less than manufacturing economies, can be highly mechanized and can provide high wages. But commodity-exporting economies in the Americas, Africa, and Asia, like that of Texas, have often been trapped in low productivity growth as a result of the low wages made possible by abundant unskilled or semi-skilled labor:

> Since there was little pressure from labour for higher wages, the entrepreneur had no interest in replacing his labour by capital or in improving the skills of his workforce. The same arguments

applied to land where it was in abundant supply. . . . Since low wages meant low productivity, the cheap labour policy became self-justifying, and through the vicious circle of low wages and low productivity, the productivity of the indigenous workforce even in thinly populated countries was fossilized at its very low initial level. *It was the pattern of low wages and productivity perpetuated by the cheap labour policy of the mines and plantations, rather than primary production as such,* which accounted for the failure of exports in underdeveloped countries to be a leading sector initiating growth in the rest of the economy. (emphasis added)[19]

The relationship between wages and mechanization is not a controversial, left-wing idea; on the contrary, it is an illustration of classical free-market economics. But to a traditional Southern conservative, the idea that high wages, by stimulating investment in technology, might enhance long-term productivity even in commodity sectors like farming, ranching, oil, and mining is as incomprehensible as quantum physics.

George W. Bush has boasted that he is the first president of the United States to have a Master of Business Administration degree. At Harvard Business School, he appears to have majored in Southernomics. For example, as governor George W. Bush opposed efforts in Texas to prevent illegal immigrants from using public services like education and health care paid for by law-abiding tax-payers. Needless to say, those taxpayers, when they subsidize poor foreign workers who have violated American immigration laws, are also subsidizing farmers, ranchers, the owners of restaurants and sweatshops, and other employers of "wetback" labor. Bush explained his support for public subsidies for illegal immigrants on the grounds that "there are a lot of jobs people in Texas won't do—laying tar in August or chopping cedars."[20] The idea that laying tar and clearing cedar could be highly mechanized and automated industries, carried out by well-paid middle-class American citizens with health care benefits and pensions, in conditions that minimize danger and discomfort, is as alien to members of the traditionalist business elite like Bush as the idea that Southern textile mills could continue to operate even if child labor was banned was to their predecessors in 1900.

The very term "bracero" says a lot about the pre-industrial mind-set of Southern conservatives like Bush and Gramm and DeLay and Armey—as well as their counterparts in much of the Latin American elite. The word is derived from the Spanish word "arm," as in the original name of the river that runs through George W. Bush's adopted county of McLennan, Texas, the Brazos de Dios, or Arms of God. A bracero is someone who works with his arms, not with his brain. There is no word in Spanish for someone who works with his brain—or in the Texan dialect of English.

The powerful hold of plantation economics on the imagination of the Southern right explains the prominent role of Texan conservatives in a controversy over a little-known U.S. protectorate called Saipan. Taken from Japan in 1944, this cluster of islands—formally known as the Commonwealth of the Northern Mariana Islands—had 27,000 inhabitants who were granted U.S. citizenship in 1986. In the 1980s, companies owned by Chinese in Hong Kong and the People's Republic of China sought to exploit the fact that products made in this U.S. protectorate could be shipped to the United States without the imposition of U.S. quotas or duties—and could even be labeled "Made in U.S.A." To exploit this loophole in American law, the Chinese businessmen set up textile factories on the islands and imported poor workers from the Philippines and Bangladesh.

In the new sweatshops, workers who lived in barracks behind barbed wire guarded by armed soldiers toiled to cut and stitch cloth for Levi Strauss, the Gap, Tommy Hilfiger, and other designer labels. When the Clinton administration sought to improve conditions for workers in Saipan by imposing a minimum wage and other reforms, the government of the islands spent millions to bring Tom DeLay, Dick Armey, and other American politicians, lobbyists, and staffers to visit, play golf, and snorkel. At a reception hosted by Willie Tan, a Chinese garment tycoon, DeLay praised the island state as an example of free enterprise, and concluded on a note of Southern-style piety that must have seemed odd to the Asian businessmen: "Stand firm. Resist evil. Remember that all truth and blessings emanate from our Creator."

The Saipan "model" is as mesmerizing to the contemporary American right as the Cuban and Soviet "models" had been to an earlier generation of the American socialist left. For DeLay, Armey, and other conservatives, Saipan illustrated the reforms that they wanted to impose on the mainland United States: the elimination of the minimum wage, and the elimination or reduction of limits on immigration and the rights of immigrant workers. The fact that this right-wing version of a "workers' paradise" resembled a slave or coolie plantation did not trouble these representatives from the old Confederacy.[21]

Island tax havens as well as island sweatshops fired the imaginations of the Republican right. One of Treasury Secretary Paul O'Neill's priorities in the first few years of the Bush administration was to cancel U.S. cooperation with other countries seeking to regulate the international tax havens in which U.S. corporations hide tens of billions of dollars to evade U.S. taxation.[22]

In the late nineteenth and early twentieth centuries, the French painter Paul Gauguin and the American anthropologist Margaret Mead, author of *Coming of Age in Samoa* (1928), had taught titillated Westerners to imagine the islands of the South Pacific as paradises of uninhibited sex. In the last decade of the twentieth century, Texan conservatives in Washington, too, dreamed of tropical islands. They dreamed of Caribbean tax havens and Pacific sweatshops—a cultural memory, perhaps, of the Atlantic islands where plantation slavery first began.

———————

In the years before George W. Bush's administration announced its unwillingness to take action against offshore tax havens, one Houston-based energy company used more than 800 dummy corporations to hide billions in assets in the Caribbean—permitting it to avoid tax liability for four of the five years previous to its bankruptcy in 2001. The company's name was Enron.[23]

The bankruptcy of Enron was the biggest corporate bankruptcy in American history. The lives of millions of employees and investors were ruined. More consequential were the repercussions from the collapse. As the public became aware that the deceptive accounting practices that led to Enron's failure were commonplace, even among seemingly-solid "blue-chip" corporations, the confidence of investors in American business plummeted. The puncturing of the tech bubble in 2000–2001 was followed in 2002 by something more serious: a withdrawal of funds from stocks by investors who might not return to the stock market for years or even decades. The collapse of Enron led to the most dramatic regulation of corporations and audit firms since the backlash against Wall Street in the early years of the New Deal.

The Enron-inspired meltdown of the U.S. stock market was bad news for President George W. Bush. "In retrospect," the noted political analyst Kevin Phillips wrote in 2002, "it's unclear whether the Bush dynasty built Enron or vice versa."[24] The close connection between the Bush family and Enron began in 1988, when president-elect Bush lobbied the government of Argentina on behalf of the company. Enron's CEO Kenneth Lay co-chaired the 1990 J-7 economic summit and joined President Bush's Export Council; as co-chairman of Bush's reelection campaign, Lay served as chairman of the host committee of the Republican Convention in Houston. After Bush was defeated by Bill Clinton, two senior members of the Bush administration—former Commerce Secretary Robert A. Mosbacher and former Secretary of State Jim Baker—were hired by Enron, which also gave a job as a company director to Texas Senator Phil Gramm's wife Wendy. Previously Wendy Gramm had been chair of the Bush administration's Commodity Futures Trading Commission, which in 1992 created a legal exemption that enriched Enron by permitting it to trade energy derivatives; after she became an Enron company director, her husband the Texas senator—who had received $100,000 from Enron in campaign contributions—supported laws in 2000 that exempted the Houston company from important financial reporting requirements.

Along with much else, George W. Bush inherited Enron from his father. As governor of Texas, Bush lobbied Pennsylvania Governor Tom Ridge on behalf of Enron. In the words of Enron CEO Ken Lay, "I said that it would be very helpful to Enron, which is obviously a huge company in the state of Texas, if he could just call the governor [of Pennsylvania] and tell him [Enron] is a serious company, this is a professional company, a good company."[25] Enron's shareholders, employees, and the world soon learned how "serious," "professional," and "good" a company Enron was. Lay became one of the son's top fund-raisers during his successful campaign for the Texas governorship and was appointed to chair Bush's Business Council. In 2000, Enron was the largest corporate contributor to the Bush presidential campaign. Vice-President Dick Cheney, a Texas oil man like Bush (in spite of his specious Wyoming residency), was a previous shareholder in Enron who had run the Halliburton Company that built Enron Field in Houston (home of the Houston Astros). Appointed by Bush to develop a federal energy policy, Cheney devised the plan in secret consultations with Ken Lay and other oil-patch executives. Bush appointed Thomas White, who was vice-chairman of Enron Energy Services when it is alleged to have hidden $500 million in losses, to be secretary of the army. Bush's attorney general, John Ashcroft, had to recuse himself from Justice Department inquiries into the Enron scandal because of the donations he had collected from Enron when he had been a U.S. senator from Missouri. Another cloud hovered over White House Chief of Staff Karl Rove, who sold around $100,000 in Enron stock only a few months before the company's bankruptcy.

The Texas energy conglomerate's largesse extended to Republican activists and intellectuals with close connections to the Bush White House. Enron put William Kristol, the editor of *The Weekly Standard*, which announced and advocated the "Bush Doctrine" of unilateralism and uncritical support of Israel, on an advisory board and paid him more than $100,000. Other "Enron pundits" included Kristol's friend Irwin Stelzer, a contributor to *The Weekly Standard*, who received $50,000; *National Review* online columnist Lawrence Kudlow, who got $50,000; *New York Times* economic columnist Paul Krugman, $50,000; and *Wall Street Journal* columnist and former Reagan speechwriter Peggy Noonan, $25,000 to $50,000, according to her vague recollections.[26] As if to illustrate the cynical manipulation of religious voters by the conservative business elite, Enron hired a prominent religious right activist to promote deregulation of energy in the state of Pennsylvania. Karl Rove, the top political adviser to George W. Bush, recommended former Christian Coalition head Ralph Reed to Enron, which paid him $10,000 to $20,000 a month until the company collapsed.[27]

Dick Cheney, a career politician, became rich after going into the business sector. During Cheney's tenure as CEO of Halliburton, federal contracts increased fifteen-fold. Between August 21 and 28, 2000, weeks before Halliburton stock prices plummeted as a result of various problems, Cheney sold 660,000 shares of company stock for a total of $35 million.[28]

Like Cheney, George W. Bush transmuted political lead into financial gold. In 1986, the younger Bush had been an investor in a failing oil company with nothing going for him other than the fact that he was the son of the vice-president of the United States. His career in business took off when he sold his failing company to Harken Energy, which generously gave him stock worth $530,000, plus $200,000 in loans to buy more stock. In 1989, George W. received an invitation to join a group of investors interested in buying the Texas Rangers baseball team. From a bank with connections to his father, Bush obtained a loan on the basis of the Harken stock. In June 1990— shortly before reports of an accounting deception drove down Harken stock—Bush sold 212,000 shares of Harken and used the proceeds of the sale to pay off the Texas Rangers loan. In 1991, Bush was investigated by the SEC for being eight months late in filing stock trade disclosures. Bush, a director of Harken, had made a fortune by unloading Harken stock just before it collapsed; the timing produced accusations, denied by Bush, that he had enriched himself by profiting from inside knowledge about the company's bad financial situation. When the SEC investigated Bush's dumping of Harken stock, the head was an appointee of his father and the SEC's general counsel was the Texas lawyer who had handled the sale of the Texas Rangers to Bush and his fellow investors in 1989. As his contribution to the Texas Rangers investors team, Bush invested about $800,000 of his own money, amounting to 1.8 percent of the capital put up by the group that bought the baseball team. By the time he cashed out,

Bush's share had grown to $2.3 million. And yet Bush received $14.9 million. How did that happen? His business partners "voluntarily" gave up some of their share of the earnings to him. In the words of the journalist Michael Kelly, "His insider-status investment of $500,000, which derived from his insider-status Harken stock, which derived from his insider status as a Bush son, eventually nets him a decent-sized fortune of $14 million."[29]

The line between politics and the economy was just as vague when George W. Bush became governor of Texas. Bush altered the rules governing the endowment of the University of Texas, one of the largest in the world. The requirements that the investment of endowment funds be monitored by "a well-recognized performance measurement service" and requiring the disclosure of "all details concerning the investments made and income realized" were eliminated. Governor Bush then "privatized" or transferred $9 million of the endowment to a nonprofit company with the name of Utimco, which did not have to subject its investment decisions to public scrutiny. The chairman of Utimco, Tom Hicks, invested at least $450 million in private funds managed by business associates of Hicks, who included big-spending Republican donors.[30]

In turning political and personal connections into a simulacrum of a business career and real money, George W. Bush was following in the footsteps of his father, whom he had followed to Andover, Yale, and the White House. The elder Bush's father, Prescott Bush, a wealthy businessman who became a U.S. senator from Connecticut, had been a friend of Neil Mallon at Yale. In 1930, Mallon, whom Prescott had encouraged to take over Dresser Industries, a holding company with a few oil companies, appointed his best friend to the board of directors. In 1948, young George H. W. Bush moved to West Texas to take a job working for one of the subsidiaries of Dresser Industries, the International Derrick & Equipment Company (Ideco). Although Bush's initial duties were modest, it was clear that he would quickly move up in the company; after all, his father Prescott owned 1,900 shares of Dresser stock, and young George Herbert Walker Bush had grown up calling the president of Dresser Industries, his father's best friend at Yale and his own employer, "Uncle Neil."[31] One must go back two or more generations in the Bush family to find members who actually earned their money by their own efforts, rather than owing it to familial and political connections.

In the aftermath of the devastating Asian financial crisis of 1997–1998, when panicked foreign investors pulled their funds out of many Asian companies, many Western analysts blamed an Asian culture of "crony capitalism," symbolized by the Chinese term for "connections"—*guanxi*. The collapse of Enron and the meltdown of the American stock market in 2001–2002 following disclosures about insider trading and sweetheart deals and deceptive accounting practices suggests that *guanxi* as a concept if not a word is familiar in the United States—particularly in the Southern United States.

The critique of crony capitalism should not be confused with the familiar critique of the corruption of democratic politics by "special interests." Crony capitalism is by far the greater threat to both democracy and the market economy. Special-interest corruption is usually taken to mean the illegitimate influence in politics of businesses and whole industries that are perfectly legitimate in their own sphere of society, the market economy. If Thomas Edison buys a U.S. senator, at least Edison does so with money he earned legitimately by inventing the light bulb and making other contributions to civilization. And democracy will survive, as not all senators are for sale. Crony capitalism refers to something else: the creation, by politically connected individuals, of a simulacrum of a corporation or a facsimile of an entire business sector. While ordinary special-interest corruption preserves the distinct identity of the politician (the bought) and the businessman (the buyer), in a regime of crony capitalism, the distinction between the private sector and the public sector all but disappears. Indeed, in such a society the private business sector is not an independent, rule-governed realm of its own, but merely a subordinate fiefdom of the political and social elite.

Crony capitalism is as distinct as socialism from genuine, entrepreneurial capitalism. Workers in the old Soviet Union used to joke, "We pretend to work and they pretend to pay us." The motto of elites in a crony-capitalist regime might be: "We pretend to be business-men—when we are not pretending to be statesmen." A sound democracy with a strong private sector can survive episodes of special-interest corruption. But crony capitalism is a terrifying quagmire that threatens to undermine and absorb the very institutions of government and the market—if, indeed, those institutions ever really existed except in name in a particular backward society.

Crony capitalism, then, is the evil twin of state capitalism in developing areas like Malaysia, Mexico, and Texas, in which government, for good or bad, performs many of the functions undertaken in more conventional capitalist communities by a native entrepreneurial elite of investors and inventors. If Texan state capitalism is represented by the LCRA, Texan crony capitalism is symbolized by another enterprise that specialized in providing energy to the public: Enron.

The two biggest American companies to fall in the second year of the Bush administration, Enron and WorldCom, had headquarters, respectively, in Houston, Texas, and Clinton, Mississippi. The "good ole boy" network—the Southern cognate of *guanxi*—was not an abuse of traditional Southern capitalism; it *was* traditional Southern capitalism. As the previous chapters have shown, bourgeois capitalism is alien to Texas and other Southern states. Instead of bourgeois capitalism, there has been a rivalry between aristocratic commodity-sector capitalism, financed by private investors outside of the region, and a technocratic state capitalism that comes in both civilian and military forms. Crony capitalism is the only kind familiar to the Southern oligarchs, descendants of planters who could not balance their books and knights who despised mere trade.

The lesson of the Enron and WorldCom scandals is not that capitalism is inherently unworkable. It is that capitalism only works where there are capitalists.

Like the father from whom he inherited the White House (but not, alas, diplomatic skill), George W. Bush is a product of commodity-exporting Third World Texas, not high-tech First World Texas. He prefers playing the country gentleman on his vast plantation near rural, pious Crawford to spending time in Austin, which has been over-run by brainy scientists, engineers, and entrepreneurs from East Asia and South Asia who do not share the traditional Southern disdain for hard work and creative thought. Austin's most prominent high-tech business leader, Michael Dell, is Jewish. The diverse and cosmopolitan world of computers and biotech is as much a puzzlement to the Bushes as it is to their friends in the royal families of Saudia Arabia and Kuwait, who, like the conservative Texan elite, have used oil revenues to keep social liberalism and secularism at bay. (The Saudi elite may be better educated.)

The crony capitalism of the Bushes and their allies in the oil patch, based on nepotism and political favors, has a culture quite different from that of most fields of business. The oil industry is political in the broadest sense; personal diplomacy is involved, from negotiating leases to international relations. Although it uses advanced technology and produces a substance vital for industrial capitalism, the oil industry rewards a mind-set and skills quite unlike those of the manufacturer who makes cars or computers. The oil patch is more like the financial sector, where bluff and cunning and timing are the keys to success, rather than scientific knowledge and engineering expertise and blueprints and long-range investment and marketing plans. If the manufacturer has the soul of an engineer, the oil man, like the financier, has the soul of a gambler.

A biographer of George W. Bush describes the future president's introduction to the oil business:

> Buzz and Ralph took George W. to the county courthouses and showed him how to look up land records—to see who owned the surface and the lower levels, and where they lived. Then they trained him in the way to make a deal. It was all talk—sweet and straight. You'd go up to some rancher and tell him why you wanted a go at his land and how much you would pay. Usually, the rancher would go for the deal, because he needed the cash. But sometimes you would find a prickly rancher, and then you would have to keep bird-dogging him, or else just drop the deal and move on to another piece of land. . . . There was always another piece of land to drill.[32]

The first U.S. president of the twenty-first century was the product of an industry in which success was determined by visiting county courthouses and sweet-talking impecunious ranchers into leases— activities that have less to do with high technology than with real estate, and have not changed significantly since 1900. As fate would have it, at the beginning of the twenty-first century, thanks to rural over-representation in the U.S. electoral college, leadership of the most advanced technological economy and the top scientific society on earth had fallen to a politician with reactionary religious beliefs from the part of the country with a primitive extractive economy. As Adlai Stevenson once observed: "In America, anyone can become president. That's one of the risks you take."

FIVE

That Old Time Religion

At the beginning of the twenty-first century, American society was characterized by growing religious tolerance and pluralism and an increase in the number (10 to 15 percent) of purely secular Americans, who, if they formed a denomination, would be the second biggest denomination in the United States after the Catholic Church. According to a 2002 *Newsweek* poll, 45 percent defined the United States as "a secular nation"; only 29 percent of Americans view the United States as "a Christian nation" and only 16 percent as a "Biblical nation, defined by the Judeo-Christian tradition."[1]

Elected with a minority of the popular vote, George W. Bush reflected the religious values and views of a declining but aggressive minority among the American people: Southern "Bible belt" fundamentalists. Bush received an overwhelming majority of the votes of the shrinking minority of white Protestants and Catholics who attend church regularly and hold traditional religious beliefs. Outside of the business community, Bush's political base was concentrated among Southern "born-again" Protestants.

George W. Bush was one of them. Asked to name the philosopher who had the greatest influence on him during the 2000 Republican primary campaign, Bush replied, "Jesus Christ." Having been raised as an establishmentarian Episcopalian, Bush switched to the moderate Methodist Church of his wife Laura, then was "born again" at the age of 40, in 1986. In his book *A Charge To Keep*, George W. Bush said that his conversion "had been planted the year before, by the Rev. Billy Graham. He visited my family for a summer weekend in

Maine. . . . And what he said sparked a change in my heart. . . . Over the course of that weekend, Rev. Graham planted a mustard seed in my soul, a seed that grew over the next year. He led me to the path, and I began walking. It was the beginning of a change in my life."

No president since Jimmy Carter has been so obtrusive and insistent in sharing his religious faith and pressuring his fellow citizens to do so as well: "The true strength of America lies in the fact that we are a faithful America by and large."[2] Bush begins each day kneeling in prayer and studies a daily Bible lesson.[3]

In the early years of the Information Age, when a scientific and technological revolution was transforming civilization, one of the issues that fascinated George W. Bush was the question of whether non-Christians will go to heaven or hell. In 1993, Bush informed an Austin reporter that only people who accepted Jesus Christ as their Savior could go to heaven. In interviews with the *Houston Post* in 1994 and the *New York Times Magazine* in 1998, Bush described a conversation with his parents in the White House during his father's administration. Having recently been "born again," the younger Bush took issue with his mother's ecumenical suggestion that "Surely, God will accept others" in heaven. With a convert's zeal, George W., the redeemed alcoholic playboy, pointed to a New Testament passage that said that only Christians would go to heaven. Any other family would have let the dispute end there, but the Bushes phoned Billy Graham from the White House. According to George W., "Billy said, 'From a personal perspective, I agree with what George is saying, the New Testament has been my guide. But I want to caution you both. Don't play God. Who are you two to be God?'"[4]

Unlike his father, a mainline Protestant who never won the confidence of the religious right, Bush—whose views are those of a Protestant fundamentalist, even though he is nominally a Methodist—was preferred by the religious right to his major rival, Senator John McCain of Arizona. During the campaign for the Republican presidential nomination, Bush pandered shamelessly to the Protestant right. He spoke at Bob Jones University, an anti-Catholic institution that until recently had banned interracial dating. More often, Bush let his surrogates do the dirty work. Religious right activists working on behalf of Bush smeared former Republican Senator Warren Rudman, who is Jewish, as an anti-Christian "bigot" for criticizing the intolerance of the far right. They also denounced Senator John McCain when he met with members of the Log Cabin Republicans, a gay Republican group. When a gay Republican congressman from Arizona, having been ordered not to mention sexual issues, addressed the Republican Convention from the stage, Bush's Texas delegation removed their hats and hung their heads in prayer. Their actions resembled the demonstrations generations earlier in Democratic national conventions when Southern segregationists who opposed civil rights planks in the party platform or, in some cases, addresses to the convention by black Democrats staged walk-outs. Bush publicly supported an archaic Texas sodomy law that makes homosexuality a crime. Bush—by his own confession, a wild playboy during his 20s and 30s—also supported criminalizing abortion.[5]

The religious zeal of George W. Bush was shared by other leading conservatives. Tom DeLay, the U.S. representative from Houston who was the House majority whip, told the congregation at First Baptist Church of Pearland, Texas, on April 2, 2002, former President Clinton had to be impeached because he had "the wrong worldview." DeLay reassured the Baptists that God was using him to promote "a biblical worldview" in American politics. He warned the congregation to send its children to schools where they could obtain a "godly education."* This kind of talk had become familiar among Republican politicians following the Southern takeover of the party in the 1980s and 1990s. In 1994, at a religious conference in Florida entitled "Reclaiming America," the first President Bush's vice-president, Dan Quayle, joined the audience in reciting a frightening theocratic parody of the Pledge of Allegiance: "I pledge allegiance to the Christian

---

*DeLay, who had been expelled as an undergraduate from Baylor Baptist university for misbehavior, claimed that Baylor and another Texan university known for its conservatism, Texas A&M, were corrupted by liberalism: "Don't send your kids to Baylor. And don't send your kids to A&M." One has to be pretty far to the right to consider Baylor and Texas A&M to be centers of godless secular humanism.

flag, and to the Savior, for whose Kingdom it stands. One Savior, crucified, risen and coming again, with life and liberty for all who believe."

———————————

Like so much else in the second Bush administration, the reactionary religiosity of its leader had its origins in the American South.

The South was not always the most religious part of the country. For centuries, that title was earned by New England, settled by the Puritans. In the colonial South and the early Republic, the members of the planter oligarchy tended to be high-church Anglicans/Episcopalians or post-Christian deists like Jefferson and Washington. These transplanted British gentlemen were often hostile to Methodist and Baptist preachers, who denounced such time-honored gentlemanly pursuits as drinking, gambling, and dueling.

In the early Republic, many of the poor white Southerners in the countryside, particularly in Appalachia and the Ozarks, were unchurched. Circuit preachers and revivals were rare, and many could not read the Bible because they were illiterate. Pagan British folk magic survived among the hill people until recent generations.

The imagery of the "country church" notwithstanding, evangelical Protestantism deepened its hold on the South as a result of urbanization and industrialization. Regular churchgoing, rare in parts of the frontier South, became more common as more Southerners lived first in small towns and then in cities. In the twentieth century, Protestant fundamentalists mastered modern organizational techniques and technology to create a flourishing subculture, based on suburban megachurches, televangelism, and chains of Christian bookstores. Much of the money that the New Deal modernizers put into the pockets of the Southern white majority ended up in the collection plates of the Southern Baptist Convention and other Protestant denominations, where it supported the lavish lifestyles of preachers who denounced New Deal liberalism.

The nineteenth-century North was as suffused with Protestant religiosity as the South in the twentieth and twenty-first centuries. But Northern Protestantism differed from Southern Protestantism in an important respect. The major difference between Northern and Southern Protestantism had to do with interpretations of the Book of Revelation, which speaks of a thousand-year reign of peace on earth. Since the Reformation, Protestants who have treated this as a literal prophecy have been divided between premillennialists and postmillennialists. Premillennialists believe that the millennium will occur only after the Second Coming of Jesus; postmillennialists, that Jesus will return to earth at the end of the millennium.

This obscure theological dispute had profound implications for American politics. The postmillennialists have tended to believe that human beings, by means of social reform, can "hasten the millennium" by their own efforts. The Kingdom of God on earth will be established by human beings, with divine inspiration but not divine power. By contrast, the premillennialists have believed that the world will get progressively worse until it is destroyed in the battle of Armageddon. Only then will Jesus descend to earth, as a literal dictator, and establish a utopian world by his own command. Premillennial Protestantism, then, tends to be indifferent to, or hostile to, social reform. What is the point of reforming an evil world that is only going to worsen until it is annihilated—perhaps in the near future?

While the seventeenth-century New England Puritans had been grim premillennialists, expecting the world to end at any moment, most of their descendants in the Northern states became optimistic postmillennialists. Throughout the nineteenth century, New Englanders and settlers from New England in the Midwest and the Pacific coast collaborated with Enlightenment Deists and secularists to promote a variety of social reforms, including the abolition of slavery, temperance, public education, and women's rights. Premillennial Southeners—in the antebellum era, no less than today—tended to denounce all social reforms as Satan-inspired schemes that provided further evidence of the decline and imminent end of the world.[6]

In the twentieth century, the religious divide between the South and the rest of the country grew broader and deeper. By the 1900s, Anglo-American Protestants were a minority in many Northern states, where great numbers of European Catholics and Jews had arrived. Because of its divisive nature, overt religiosity ceased to be part of mainstream political culture in the diverse communities of the Northeast, Midwest, and West Coast. The absence of significant Catholic and Jewish immigration to the South, by contrast, permitted the Anglo-Celtic Southern majority to continue to equate the American way of life with Bible-believing Protestantism.

In addition, Northern and Southern Protestantism responded to advances in scientific knowledge in the twentieth century in ways that made them ever more unlike. Until the middle of the nineteenth century, Protestant theologians had been able to argue that natural science was compatible with the account of creation and world history found in the Bible. This argument was demolished by Darwin, who revealed that the evolution of life and animal consciousness could be completely accounted for by the operation of random processes on matter, without the action of a supernatural creator. Northern Protestants responded by becoming more or less openly secular, or by reinterpreting the Bible as an allegory.

The other response was fundamentalism—a Protestant theological movement of the early twentieth century that resisted any compromise with modern science or scholarship. While the fundamentalist movement was nationwide, its basis soon became the Protestant South. The Scopes trial of 1925, in which former U.S. Secretary of State and Populist presidential candidate William Jennings Bryan prosecuted a public schoolteacher under a Tennessee statute that banned the teaching of Darwinian biology, confirmed the image in the North and the world of the South as a land of ignorant bumpkins. The ridicule only strengthened the Southern fundamentalists, who added anti-Darwinian creationism to the Lost Cause myth of the Confederacy and white supremacy as part of their parochial belief system.

Hostile to the world and encapsulated in its own subcultural network of institutions, Southern Protestant fundamentalism at the beginning of the twenty-first century had hardly changed from the 1920s, when it took on its present form. Beginning in the 1970s, Jerry Falwell's Moral Majority and later Pat Robertson's Christian Coalition mobilized the so-called religious right—really the white Southern Protestant fundamentalist right, most of whom in previous generations had been conservative Democrats. Although genuine fundamentalists amount to no more than around 5 percent of the U.S. population, the high turnout of religious-right activists in Republican primary elections allowed them to capture the Republican Party by the 1990s. As these ex-Democratic Southern fundamentalists hijacked the GOP, growing numbers of Republicans in the Northeast, Midwest, and West Coast quit the party in disgust, becoming Democrats or independents.

While the Southern Protestant fundamentalists dominated the Republican Party at the level of activists and voters, they were under-represented among Republican policy experts, intellectuals, academics, and journalists. The reason was obvious: anti-intellectual cultures, like that of the fundamentalist South, do not produce world-class, or even national-class, intellectuals.

Incapable of producing intellectuals of its own, the Southern right borrowed some from the East Coast left. In the 1980s and 1990s, Southern Protestant fundamentalists found intellectual allies among the "neoconservatives." Like the Southern conservatives, and unlike the old Republican elites, the neoconservatives had been Democrats who switched to the Republican Party following the leftward lurch of the Democrats in the 1960s. Most were first- or second-generation Jewish-Americans, but a few were Catholic or mainline Protestant. Most in practice were secular; their religious affiliation, if any, was a matter of ethnicity rather than of devout belief. In their outlook as well as their backgrounds, these secular Northeastern intellectuals, often educated in, or employed by, Ivy League universities, could not have been more unlike the "Bible-believing Christians" of the American South.

At first the neoconservative-fundamentalist alliance was limited to the shared goal of supporting Israel against its critics (this aspect of the alliance will be discussed in detail in the following chapter). Over time, however, the leading neoconservatives like Irving Kristol, editor of *The Public Interest,* and his son William Kristol, editor of *The Weekly Standard,* gradually adopted the views of the Southern religious right on social policy, like opposition to abortion and gay rights, hostility to biotechnology, and support for government subsidies to religious schools. The rightward drift of the neoconservative movement led many prominent moderate neoconservatives, like Daniel Patrick Moynihan, Daniel Bell, Peter Berger, and Samuel P. Huntington, to distance themselves from it or sever their ties.

By the year 2000, a Frankensteinian operation stitched the bodiless head of Northeastern neoconservatism onto the headless body of Southern fundamentalism. Neoconservative intellectuals like William Kristol and William Bennett sought to translate the beliefs of the Southern fundamentalists who controlled the Republican Party into the language of mainstream American policy debate. Cynics interpreted this as hypocritical opportunism. When Baptist voters elected Republican presidents, the good jobs in Washington went, not to Baptist appointees, but to Ivy League-educated Jewish, Catholic, and mainline Protestant neoconservatives.

The neoconservative intellectuals defended their opportunistic alliance with the anti-intellectual Southern fundamentalists with an ingenious rationale. This was the argument that American politics was characterized by a "culture war" between religion and secular humanism, which some neoconservatives quaintly called "irreligion." In this struggle, the neoconservatives argued, religious Protestants, Catholics, and Jews had to set aside their theological differences in order to unite against the forces of irreligion.

While this theory was useful in justifying the alliance of ambitious East Coast apparatchiks with Deep South voters, it suffered from fatal flaws. To begin with, ordinary Protestant fundamentalists continued to believe that Catholics were not genuine Christians and that Jews, Muslims, Hindus, Buddhists, and secularists would burn in hell for eternity unless they converted to Christianity. The Christian Coalition's attempt to create a Catholic wing failed because of the anti-Catholic bigotry of the fundamentalists. And the enduring racial prejudices of Southern fundamentalists prevented them from winning over black Protestants, whose religious views were similar to their own.

What is more, few of the neoconservatives who filled positions in the executive branch, Congress, Washington think tanks, or political magazines could be distinguished, in their personal lives, from ordinary

secularists who engaged in premarital sex and took advantage of the legality of contraception and abortion. While devout Protestant fundamentalists tried to live according to their beliefs, most neoconservatives preached moral conservatism while they practiced moral liberalism.

Philosophical justification for their hypocrisy was provided for many neoconservatives by the teachings of Leo Strauss, an influential German Jewish émigré professor at the University of Chicago who influenced many neoconservative thinkers, including Irving Kristol and the late Allan Bloom. Strauss distinguished the "philosophers," a tiny elite capable of apprehending philosophical wisdom, and the masses, whose primitive minds could comprehend only traditional religions like Judaism and Christianity. Rather than provoke the masses, who might kill the philosophers as the Athenian mob had executed Socrates, the philosophic elite should keep its advanced views to itself. This rationale permitted Straussian neoconservatives to despise the beliefs of Southern Baptists in private, while defending fundamentalist policies toward abortion, gay rights, and biotechnology in public debate. They were not hypocrites; they were "philosophers."

But not all neoconservatives were cynical, ambitious office-seekers, hoping to ride to power and celebrity in Washington on the shoulders of stampeding Southern Baptists. For some former leftists and liberals on the neoconservative right, what was at first an alliance of convenience with Southern Protestants grew into an alliance of conviction. An example of this was an address given in 1996 by Gertrude Himmelfarb, an academic historian and the wife of Irving Kristol, known as "the godfather of the neoconservatives," as well as the mother of William Kristol, whose Washington-based magazine, *The Weekly Standard,* funded by the Australian media tycoon Rupert Murdoch, became the leading political magazine of the neoconservatives. Like her husband, Himmelfarb had begun on the left but had migrated far to the right. In 1995, Himmelfarb wrote the preface for a book published by the New York-based conservative magazine *National Review,* entitled *This Will Hurt: The Restoration of Virtue and Civic Order*. The sadistic authoritarianism of the title was echoed in the titles of essays like "Ostracism and Disgrace in the Maintenance of a Precarious Social Order" and "Administering Punishment Morally, Publicly, and Without Excuse" (this might have been particularly popular in Texas, which had led the nation in executions in recent years). In her preface, Himmelfarb called for a crackdown: "It is evident that we are suffering from a grievous moral disorder. . . . And that moral pathology requires strenuous moral purgatives and restoratives."[7]

The title of Himmelfarb's address at Baylor Baptist University in 1996 was "The Christian University: A Call to Counterrevolution." For a secular Jewish intellectual to praise a Christian university was odd, to say the least. Even odder was her version of intellectual history. In the mid-twentieth century, the largely-Jewish "New York Intellectuals" from whose ranks neoconservatives like the Kristols had emerged had found a model of enlightened and humane intelligence in Matthew Arnold, the subject of a biography by Lionel Trilling. But Arnold's idea of high culture, Himmelfarb told her Protestant fundamentalist audience at Baylor, was largely responsible for what was wrong with modern education:

> Indeed, it was the idea of "culture"—a secular, rational, cosmopolitan, liberal (in the nonpolitical sense of that word) culture—far more than the idea of "science," that lay behind the secularization of the university in the late-nineteenth and early-twentieth centuries. There were even educators and intellectuals—"humanists," they proudly called themselves—who thought that science (or too heavy a dose of science) was as inimical to a liberal education as was religion (or too sectarian a religion). Matthew Arnold's famous definition of culture, "the best which might have been thought and said in the world," was endorsed by Irving Babbitt, Charles Eliot Norton, and other luminaries of American intellectual life.

The Baptists in Texas, long accustomed to hearing their pastors denounce Charles Darwin for his contributions to modern science, were now being invited by a leading Jewish intellectual to despise another great nineteenth-century British thinker, Matthew Arnold, for his influence on the idea of culture. If Himmelfarb was to be believed, under the influence of Matthew Arnold and Charles Eliot Norton, American universities "with a few notable exceptions, Baylor University being one of them—succumbed to the spirit of the times" in the late nineteenth century—that is, they ceased being sectarian Christian colleges and became secular universities with freedom of thought and opinion. "That was the first reformation in the university: the disestablishment of the church," said Himmelfarb, making her disapproval of "the disestablishment of the church" clear. She argued that "a university like Baylor, respectful of religion and of the moral virtues derived from religion, can serve as a powerful corrective to the secular university." Religious dogma should be the basis of universities, as in the old days of established churches and sectarian colleges: "It is a propitious time, therefore, for a university like Baylor, which has kept faith with its religious and ethical heritage, to contemplate a counterrevolution that will restore the original academic dogma and make the university once again a repository of intellectual and moral virtue."[8]

Himmelfarb probably had not read the initial Baylor University catalogue of 1886, but she would have been pleased to learn that it subordinated thought to dogma: "The study of philosophy and logic as taught in this department is not to familiarize the student with the learned but now exploded theories of past ages, but to prepare every student to become a true patriot and devoted Christian."[9] Of Baylor University, which Himmelfarb held up as a model of higher education, the Waco editor William Cowper Brann, before he was shot in the back and mortally wounded by an enraged Baptist citizen of Waco, had written in the 1890s: "It is the Alma Mater of mob violence. It is a chronic breeder of bigotry and bile."[10]

While neoconservative intellectuals provided the rationalizations, Southern fundamentalists provided the agenda for George W. Bush in social policy. An example is the central social policy initiative of Bush's presidency: the transfer of government responsibilities for welfare to "faith-based institutions."

The mastermind of Bush's faith-based public policy initiative was an eccentric figure named Marvin Olasky, a journalism teacher at the University of Texas. Like many neoconservatives, Olasky was an ex-leftist Christian convert. Born Jewish, the son of a Hebrew teacher in Boston, Olasky flirted with communism before converting to Protestant fundamentalism.

Olasky held bizarre "biblical" views about women. In a newspaper article about the biblical story of Deborah and Barak, the Jewish Bostonian-cum-Texan Protestant fundamentalist explained, "God does not forbid women to be leaders in society, generally speaking. As in the situation of Deborah and Barak, there's a certain shame attached. I would vote for a woman for the presidency, in some situations, but again, there's a certain shame attached. Why don't you have a man who's able to step forward?" Bush's domestic policy guru at the University of Texas Journalism School wrote this around the time that the Southern Baptist Convention declared that women should "graciously submit" to their husbands.

The Heritage Foundation, a right-wing think tank in Washington, and the conservative Bradley Foundation funded his book, *The Tragedy of American Compassion* (1992), in which he argued for abandoning twentieth-century government welfare programs and turning over responsibility for the poor and needy to Christian charities and other religious institutions. Tendentious and inaccurate, Olasky's tract was dismissed by serious scholars, but leading Washington conservatives like Bill Bennett and Newt Gingrich—who compared Olasky to Alexis de Tocqueville—treated the tract as a blueprint for a new conservative social policy. George W. Bush claimed to be influenced by Olasky, and promoted the sharing of government funds for welfare programs with religious groups, even before he ran for president on the slogan of "compassionate conservatism" (a phrase that Olasky and Republican operatives devised).

The phrase "compassionate conservatism" disguised Olasky's radical goal: a rejection of the American tradition of separation of church and state, which he believes was a mistake, in favor of a return to the seventeenth- and eighteenth-century colonial tradition of established churches in the British American colonies. "Maybe disestablishment wasn't such a good idea," Olasky has suggested. Writing in the *Austin American Statesman* on July 5, 2000, Olasky denounced James Madison for supporting the disestablishment of religion in Virginia in the 1780s and praised Patrick Henry for proposing a "multiple establishment" of religion with his 1785 "Bill Establishing a Provision for Teachers of the Christian Religion." At least Olasky was honest enough to recognize that Madison, Jefferson, Washington, and other leading Founders were opposed to what he and the contemporary religious right want to do; many conservative Christians simply falsify history and claim that the American Founders (many of whom were deists or unitarians) were devout Protestants like themselves.

As a model of a faith-based leader, Bush held up former Watergate criminal and born-again evangelical Protestant Charles Colson. "Charles Colson's Prison Fellowship ministry comes to mind," Bush answered, when asked about faith-based organizations.[11] The example of Colson is disturbing. In a 1997 issue of *Christianity Today*, Charles Colson published an article entitled "Can We Still Pledge Allegiance?"[12] Then in November 1996, Colson and Robert Bork published pieces critical of the federal judiciary in an issue of *First Things*, in which the editors toyed with treason, asking "whether we have reached or are reaching the point where conscientious citizens can no longer give moral assent to the existing regime" and comparing the United States to Nazi Germany. Sounding like a member of the militia movement, Colson wrote in the same issue: "We dare not at present despair of America and advocate open rebellion." However, he warned, "If the terms of our contract have in fact been broken, Christian citizens may be compelled to force the government to return to its original understanding—as even Enlightenment rationalists have acknowledged." By this he meant a return to the seventeenth-century Calvinist Puritan understanding of America, which many on the Protestant right believe was rejected by immoral "Enlightenment rationalists" such as Thomas Jefferson and Benjamin Franklin.

As governor of Texas, George W. Bush successfully persuaded the Texas legislature to pass a bill that permitted faith-based institutions to opt out of state licensing requirements. Mainstream Christian and Jewish organizations had never objected to state licensing; the major witness during hearings in the Texas House of Representatives was the attorney for the Roloff Homes, a facility for delinquent children run by a fundamentalist evangelist named Lester Roloff. In the 1970s and 1980s, the state of Texas had repeatedly tried to force Roloff to submit to state licensing and oversight. The state shut down his Rebekah Home in 1985; in 1974, a state judge sent Roloff to jail for five days for contempt of court.

Roloff found political allies in Republican governors—first Bill Clements, then George W. Bush. Thanks to Bush's support, the Texas legislature permitted Roloff to reopen his Rebekah Home for delinquent girls in 1999. In *Texas Monthly,* Pamela Colloff described the horrifying ordeal of one 16-year-old girl who was left by her mother with Roloff's staff at the Rebekah Home, which resembled a rural concentration camp. After the girl refused to write "I will not talk in class" one hundred times, she was thrown into the "lockup":

> Inside the lockup, Lester Roloff's voice began to play over the intercom, his rich baritone echoing off the walls—sermonizing, singing gospel songs, and exhorting all who listened to come to Jesus. His voice droned on as morning turned into afternoon and afternoon into evening. . . . She began kicking the wall that night, and by morning a hole had formed in the Sheetrock. ("I felt like I was losing my mind," she said.) Mrs. Cameron warned her that if she did not stop, she would be restrained. When DeAnne persisted, she was wrestled to the ground by three male guards, who pinned her arms behind her back while Mrs. Cameron bound her wrists with duct tape. Her ankles were then bound as well, and once she was immobilized, someone—DeAnne is unsure who—gave her a hard kick to the ribs. She was left alone to writhe on the floor, gasping for air.[13]

Her confinement in the "lockup" by these religious zealots lasted for thirty-two hours. She was fortunate; one girl was confined to the lockup for a month. Other forms of punishment at the Rebekah Home included "kneeling" (kneeling for hours with a Bible in each hand, with pencils wedged under the knees) and "sitting on the wall" (sitting against a wall without a chair). The punishments meted out by these religious-right supporters of George W. Bush to children in their care resemble some of the tortures inflicted on American prisoners of war in Vietnam and Korea.

As a result of incidents like these, the Texas legislature—defying the wishes of George W. Bush—refused to renew the law exempting faith-based child care facilities from state oversight.* Undeterred, Bush made the relaxation of federal standards for organizations like Lester Roloff's the centerpiece of his social policy as president. However, Bush's faith-based policy initiative withered in Washington, D.C., after it was revealed that Bush's top aide, Karl Rove, had secretly negotiated with the Salvation Army to exempt religious organizations receiving federal funds from state and local anti-discrimination laws. John DiIulio, the respected sociologist who headed the project, resigned; a Catholic, he was distrusted by many Protestant fundamentalists who believe that Catholics are not "Bible-believing Christians." To make matters worse, many white Southern preachers lost interest in the initiative when it became clear that much of the federal money would flow to black urban churches in the Northern cities. In short, the faith-based initiative—the favorite domestic policy initiative of the Protestant right—collapsed because of the anti-Catholic and anti-black prejudices of Bush's Southern fundamentalist supporters.

Southern Protestant fundamentalists were also responsible for the major Bush administration initiative in the area of science and technology: the attempted outlawing of embryonic stem cell research.

Many scientists believe that embryonic stem cells, which can grow into any organ or tissue, have the potential to transform medicine and prolong longevity by permitting organs to be replaced by new ones which, grown from the patient's own cells, would not be rejected

---

*In the early 1980s, when I worked as an aide for the Texas Senate in Austin, Brother Lester called upon God to put a curse on the Texas legislature. This would explain a great deal about the legislature.

by the patient's body. The new organs would be grown from the stem cells in an embryo created when one of the patient's cells, such as a skin cell, is implanted in a female ovum. This procedure is known as therapeutic cloning, because the embryo would be a potential twin of the patient. Rather than being allowed to grow into a much-younger twin, however, the embryo, when it was still no more than a microscopic clump of cells, would provide versatile stem cells and then be destroyed.

Human embryos are created and discarded in the laboratory routinely, as part of fertility-clinic treatments for infertility. For most Americans, as for most of the inhabitants of Europe and Asia, therapeutic cloning is no more troubling than artificial insemination. However, there is an international consensus against reproductive cloning, which would allow laboratory-created clones to grow beyond the embryonic stage and mature into babies. Some of the few cloned animals that were not destroyed by miscarriage have suffered terrible birth defects.

Most democracies in Europe and East Asia permit therapeutic cloning, subject to stringent government regulation, while banning reproductive cloning. If the Confederacy had won its war of independence, and if the southern border of the United States were the Mason-Dixon Line, this would almost certainly be the regime in the United States today. However, the South is part of the United States. And the South is full of Protestant fundamentalists who believe that embryos—even embryos created in the laboratory, by the injection of a skin cell into a hollow ovum—are babies. The same religious belief that leads the Southern right to oppose abortion leads its members to oppose therapeutic cloning of embryos for stem cell production, along with in vitro fertilization for infertile couples. Some fundamentalists have even suggested that embryos created by fertility clinics be protected by law and implanted in female volunteers.

After assuming the presidency, George W. Bush supported the Human Cloning Prohibition Act, which the Republican House of Representatives passed in 2001. The bill prescribed civil penalties with fines of no less than $1 million and a criminal penalty of up to ten years in prison for medical researchers, doctors, and patients.

Americans who traveled to other countries with more lenient regimes and received drugs or medical treatments using stem cells derived from cloning were threatened with bankrupting fines and even jail time. Fortunately, the Senate version of this extreme bill, introduced by Kansas Republican Sam Brownback, was blocked in Congress by the Democrats who controlled that body following the defection of the moderate Republican Senator Jim Jeffords in 2001. Most Democrats, and some moderate Republicans, preferred to follow the example of other advanced industrial democracies in outlawing reproductive cloning while making therapeutic cloning legal but subject to government regulation.

Unable to persuade Congress to ban therapeutic cloning, Bush used his power over the executive branch to limit government subsidies for stem cell research to research efforts that used only embryos created before August 9, 2001. This compromise muddied the principle—if embryos are little people, why should those created before a certain date be allowed to be destroyed?—and the decision applied only to research funded by the federal government, not to privately funded research. Still, Bush's decision was a victory for the religious right. In the months that followed, most scientists argued that the number of stem cell "lines" available for research was far smaller than Bush had claimed. Some prominent American scientists even moved to Britain, Singapore, and other countries where there was no threat to biomedical research from Southern-style religious fundamentalists.

The anti-intellectualism of the Texan right was influenced by social inequality in Texas, as well as by Protestant fundamentalism. Like many Southern states, Texas had a school system tailored to a hierarchical class and caste system. Its leading universities, like the University of Texas at Austin, Southern Methodist University (SMU), and Rice University, were world-class. Or, to be more specific, "planter class." As the historian Raimondo Luraghi has observed, "Throughout the colonial Americas (usually considered a wilderness by contemporary Europeans), the planter classes boasted a very high standard of sophisticated culture: they spoke French, Italian, and other languages; kept good libraries where Latin and Greek authors were to be found; and sent their children to study in Europe."[14] The purpose of traditional Southern higher education was to turn the children of the rich and affluent into the well-read and sophisticated politicians, lawyers, business directors, and ministers who would run the society in the next generation. The majority of the population, doomed by birth to menial agricultural or domestic labor or semi-skilled industry, needed no more than basic literacy and numeracy—if they even needed that. During the decades of "separate but equal" education for blacks and whites in Texas, the schools for most white Texans, although better-funded and better-equipped than the black schools, were grossly inferior by the standards of the Northern states or other industrial democracies.

In 1984, in response to a lawsuit over educational inequity that was working its way through the state court system, Governor Mark White, a centrist Democrat, appointed Ross Perot to head a commission on how to reform Texas public education. More than any other individual, Perot was responsible for revolutionary reforms of the Texas public schools in the last two decades of the twentieth century. Like other corporate leaders in the tech sector, Perot understood that the key resource needed to promote Texan prosperity in the future is the gray matter of the brain—not the black soil of the East Texas river valleys or the black gold of the West Texas oil fields.

The Perot commission proposed a package of dramatic reforms, including small class sizes, expanded kindergarten programs, and testing to make schools accountable. The Perot reforms encountered resistance from the left, by black and Latino activists who complained that non-white students would disproportionately fail tougher tests. But the greatest opposition came from small-town white Texans, who were shocked by the commission's proposed "no-pass, no-play" rule (high school football players who did not pass all of their courses would be kicked off the school football team). Ross Perot could not have shocked Texas more if he had announced that he had converted to Marxism-Leninism.[15]

Unlike most commission reports, this one was actually enacted by a coalition of politicians, activists, and judges in which enlightened business leaders in the advanced part of the Texas economy played a major role. While the actual degree to which Texas education improved as a result was disputed, studies by a RAND team and other scholars showed dramatic improvement in the academic performance of students in Texas by 1996.[16]

If Ross Perot did not have sufficient reasons to despise the Bush family, another was added when Governor George W. Bush, running for president in 2000, claimed responsibility for the educational reforms that were really the work of Perot and his allies in the 1980s— even though the social-science data showed that the improvement had begun before he took office. Bush's own contribution to the Texas educational debate, other than favoring school choice, was to promote "local control" of curricula. For generations, the phrase "local control" in Texas had been used as a hunting license by the Baptist Church and right-wing zealots to pressure schools and school boards to purge anything from the curricula and school libraries that promoted natural science, secularism, socialism, racial integration, environmentalism, or political liberalism. In recent decades, the censorship campaign was led by Mel and Norma Gabler, a conservative couple from East Texas who, with support from the national religious right, sought to ensure that all textbooks used in Texas public schools promoted their notions of traditional Christian morality and belief, conservative patriotism, support for free-market capitalism, and hostility to environmental science.[17] In one textbook hearing, far-right activists complained that a textbook about slavery was guilty of "overkill of emphasis on cruelty to slaves."[18]

Since the nineteenth century, opposition to the teaching of "Darwinism"—that is to say, modern biology—has been a priority of the Protestant fundamentalists in Texas and similar states. Until the 1990s, this was not a traditional theme of the national Republican Party. But the domination of the Republican primaries by fundamentalist voters had made ritual denunciation of Darwin a necessity for Republican candidates for the presidential nomination. In 2000, Gary Bauer declared that he refuses to teach his children that they are "descendant from apes," while Malcolm "Steve" Forbes accused textbooks about evolution of perpetrating "a massive fraud."[19]

While campaigning for president in 2000, George W. Bush announced on one occasion that "on the issue of evolution, the verdict is still out on how God created the earth." On another occasion he expressed his support for the teaching in schools of pseudoscientific, Biblically inspired "creation science" or "intelligent design theory," pseudosciences that bear the relation to genuine biology that alchemy does to chemistry and that astrology does to astrophysics: "I have no problem explaining that there are different theories about how the world was formed. I mean, after all, religion has been around a lot longer than Darwinism."[20] One of his predecessors in the White House, Woodrow Wilson, asked in 1912 about his views on evolution, replied "that of course like every other man of intelligence and education I do believe in organic evolution. It surprises me that at this late date such questions should be raised." Also in 1912, ex-President Theodore Roosevelt, in a speech delivered to the American Historical Association, referred to "the great Darwin." In "My Life as a Naturalist," published in *The American Museum Journal* in May 1918, Roosevelt wrote of his childhood education: "Thank Heaven, I sat at the feet of Darwin and Huxley."

But perhaps George W. Bush was right and Darwin was wrong after all. Certainly in politics there was no evidence of evolution. Between the mid-twentieth century and the beginning of the twenty-first, enlightened, dynamic Texan modernists like Lyndon Johnson, Ralph Yarborough, Maury Maverick, Sam Rayburn, and Wright Patman had been replaced in Washington, D.C., by reactionaries like George W. Bush, Tom DeLay, Dick Armey, and Phil Gramm, who combined sincere or calculated expressions of belief in Biblical inerrancy with devout service to the most primitive, resource-squandering kinds of cheap-labor commodity capitalism. Substituting Franklin Roosevelt and Lyndon Johnson for Washington and the two Bushes for Grant, one could update the classic line by Henry Adams: "The progress of evolution from President Washington to President Grant was alone evidence enough to upset Darwin."

SIX

Armageddon

In the weeks following the al-Qaeda terrorist attacks on New York and Washington, D.C., on September 11, 2001, nations across the world expressed their sympathy for the United States. The French newspaper *Le Monde*, often critical of the United States, declared "We are all Americans now." Even the anti-American clerical regime in Iran denounced the terrorists and organized public demonstrations of mourning. As an expression of solidarity, America's European allies invoked Article V of the NATO treaty, which treats an attack on one member as an attack on all, for the first time in the history of the alliance. The successful U.S. campaign to topple the Taliban regime in Afghanistan that had provided Osama bin Laden with a headquarters for his global terrorist organization won broad if not universal support. In most of the world, the United States was viewed as waging a just war in a just cause against enemies of global civilization.

By the first anniversary of the September 11 attacks, support for American foreign policy among most of America's allies had collapsed, and the American political elite was deeply divided. Having failed to pacify Afghanistan or to root out al-Qaeda operatives in neighboring Pakistan, the Bush administration was planning a war on a third front: the invasion of Iraq and the toppling of Saddam Hussein. While Congress and the international community supported UN inspections of Iraqi weapons and the disarmament of Iraq, the Bush administration's eagerness to conquer and occupy Iraq met serious opposition at home and abroad. One respected Republican foreign policy veteran after another—former National Security Adviser Brent Scowcroft; former

Secretary of State Henry Kissinger; General Norman Schwarzkopf, the military commander during the Gulf War; and General Wesley Clark, the commander of the NATO forces in Kosovo, among others— opposed or raised troubling questions about George W. Bush's Iraq plans. Meanwhile, relations between America's soldiers and the civilian political appointees at the Pentagon had deteriorated to the lowest point since the Vietnam War.

The most surprising thing about the foreign policy of George W. Bush is how little it was affected by September 11, 2001. Before the terrorist attacks, the Bush administration was busily canceling treaties and withdrawing the United States from international conventions; planning an invasion of Iraq; and treating the Likud government of Israel as its closest foreign ally. After September 11, in the name of "the war on terror," the Bush administration continued to carry out exactly the same policies—even though unilateralism, the planned invasion and occupation of Iraq, and the pro-Sharon tilt undermined America's ability to muster a long-lasting global coalition to identify and thwart the remnants of the al-Qaeda terrorist network. Indeed, on September 12, 2002, in his address to the United Nations, Bush made it clear that overthrowing Saddam Hussein—not defeating the still-dangerous al-Qaeda terrorist network—was the priority of his administration. A year after the al-Qaeda assault, the United States was more isolated abroad, and more divided over foreign policy at home, than at any time since the Vietnam War.

George Herbert Walker Bush had been derided for his lack of interest in what he memorably called "the vision thing." George W. Bush's advisers, if not Bush himself, were visionaries with visions to spare. They had a plan of what the twenty-first century world would look like, a plan almost hallucinatory in its vivid detail. The United States must maintain its status as the sole superpower by spending more on its arsenal than most of the other major military nations combined. Shrugging off international law and diplomacy, the United States would wage "pre-emptive" wars against regimes that might pose speculative threats, even if they did not threaten the United States and its allies with imminent danger. The United States would free itself from its pusillanimous British and European allies and dispatch bombs and justice in solitary grandeur everywhere except in the Middle East, where the United States would share its regional domination with Israel. This strategy broke with American foreign policy tradition, but it had the support of two groups of former Democratic constituencies: ex-leftist, mostly Jewish neoconservatives and reactionary white Southern Protestant fundamentalists. Southern conservatives in the Dixiecrat tradition, in an alliance of convenience with mostly Jewish neoconservatives, dominated the right wing of the Republican Party and controlled the foreign policy of the executive branch in the first years of the twenty-first century.

The immediate source of the foreign policy of George W. Bush can be found in the administration of his father, George Herbert Walker Bush. The leading foreign policymakers in the first Bush administration, like Secretary of State James Baker and his successor Laurence Eagleberger and Chairman of the Joint Chiefs of Staff Colin Powell, were conservative internationalists committed, like the president they served, to preserving and expanding America's alliance system. The first Bush administration sought to use the enhanced influence of the United States as the only global superpower, in the aftermath of the Cold War, to lead the world through international institutions, not to dominate the world by brute force. In the name of international law, the United States, with the sanction of the UN Security Council, led a coalition of dozens of nations to expel Iraq from Kuwait. Then, in order to avoid splitting the anti-Iraq alliance, the Bush administration chose to forego the occupation of Iraq, leaving Saddam Hussein in control of only a portion of Iraq's territory and forcing him to agree to UN weapons inspections.

Within the first Bush administration, however, a minority of high-ranking "neoconservative" policymakers had different ideas. Led by Undersecretary of Defense Paul Wolfowitz, a brilliant former academic and diplomat, and including then-Secretary of Defense Dick Cheney, this neoconservative faction was bitterly disappointed by the decision of George Herbert Walker Bush not to occupy Iraq. In the spring of 1992, then-Secretary of Defense Dick Cheney circulated, within the Bush administration, a classified draft document entitled "Defense Planning Guidance" describing America's proposed role in the world at the highest levels of the Pentagon. Drafted under the direction of Paul Wolfowitz, the report foreshadowed the themes of the strategy followed a decade later by George W. Bush: preserving American military primacy by means of massive, permanent defense spending; the pre-emptive use of military force to prevent the proliferation of weapons of mass destruction; and the downgrading of alliances and international organizations in favor of unilateral American action.

According to the Wolfowitz draft, the United States "must maintain the mechanisms for deterring potential competitors from even aspiring to a larger regional or global role." Among the "potential competitors" described were Germany and Japan, which, like China and Russia, according to Wolfowitz and Cheney, were to be deterred by American military might from assuming any larger military role in Europe or Asia. Instead, these other great powers were to be kept permanently weak and disarmed, subordinate to the United States even in their own neighborhoods. A decade before President George W. Bush listed Iraq and North Korea as part of an "axis of evil" on January 27, 2002, the Wolfowitz report suggested that pre-emptive U.S. military force might be needed to prevent them from obtaining weapons of mass destruction. Anticipating the contempt of the second Bush administration for America's allies, Wolfowitz in the first Bush administration in 1992 dismissed alliances, arguing that "we should expect future coalitions to be ad hoc assemblies, often not lasting beyond the crisis being confronted, and in many cases carrying only agreement over the objectives to be accomplished."[1]

When the draft document was leaked to the press, the result was an explosive controversy in the United States and around the world. The administration of George Herbert Walker Bush quickly distanced itself from the radicalism of the Cheney–Wolfowitz report. Deputy Secretary of State Lawrence Eagleburger and others quickly assured foreign diplomats that the unilateralist views of Cheney and Wolfowitz did not reflect American policy.

During the Clinton years, the neoconservatives were forced to watch U.S. foreign policy from the sidelines. Cheney made a fortune as head of Halliburton oil company, while Paul Wolfowitz and like-minded veterans of the first Bush administration brooded in exile in universities and think tanks. Defeated and humiliated in the first Bush administration, Paul Wolfowitz returned to the private acade-mic sector as dean of the Johns Hopkins School of Advanced Inter-national Studies (SAIS). He and his neoconservative allies spent the 1990s writing articles and making public appearances in which they argued that the decision of the United States not to take Baghdad had been a mistake. On September 17, 1998, Wolfowitz testified before the House National Security Committee on Iraq, calling for the United States to "create a liberated zone in Southern Iraq" that could trigger an unlikely Iraqi popular uprising.[2] In 1999, Wolfowitz kept up the drumbeat for war against Iraq, co-authoring a letter in the March/April issue of *Foreign Affairs* with former New York Congress-man Stephen Solarz in which he called on the United States again "to commit ground forces to protect a sanctuary in southern Iraq where the opposition could safely mobilize."[3]

In exile, Wolfowitz and his fellow neoconservatives devised their own[4] grand strategy for the United States. Its basic themes were pre-sented to the public before the 2000 election, in a book edited by William Kristol and Robert Kagan, *Present Dangers: Crisis and Oppor-tunity in American Foreign and Defense Policy* (2000).[4] The former British diplomat Jonathan Clarke observed in a review, "If the book's recommendations were implemented all at once, the U.S. would risk unilaterally fighting at least a five-front war, while simultaneously urg-ing Israel to abandon the peace process in favour of a new no-hold-barred confrontation with the Palestinians."[5] This turned out to be a prediction of the policies that the administration of George W. Bush would adopt in the following two years.

With the election of George W. Bush in 2000, the frustrated neo-conservatives finally had an opportunity to put their ambitious schemes for reordering the world into practice. In the second Bush administration, the relative influence of the neoconservatives and the realists was the opposite of the pattern in the administration of

George W. Bush's father. Conservative internationalists like Secretary of State Powell were quickly marginalized. As the number two figure at the Pentagon, under Secretary of Defense Donald Rumsfeld, Paul Wolfowitz quickly became the dominant player in the administration of George W. Bush, with the help of longtime allies like Dick Cheney, George W. Bush's vice-president, and Undersecretary of State John R. Bolton, a hardline conservative placed in the State Department as a check upon the moderate Secretary of State Colin Powell.

The adoption of the Wolfowitz Doctrine, under the title of the Bush Doctrine, as U.S. strategy was signaled on June 1, 2002, when George W. Bush delivered a graduation speech at West Point. The president echoed all of the obsessions that had swirled through the writings of Wolfowitz and his allies for a decade. First, pre-emptive wars against countries like Iraq: "If we wait for threats to fully materialize, we will have waited too long." Then, an American near-monopoly on military power worldwide: "America has, and intends to keep, military strengths beyond challenge, thereby making the destabilizing arms races of other eras pointless, and limiting rivalries to trade and other pursuits of peace." On September 20, the White House released a thirty-three-page document declaring that U.S. forces "will be strong enough to dissuade potential adversaries from pursuing a military buildup in hopes of surpassing, or equaling, the power of the United States."[6] The Wolfowitz–Bush Doctrine was now official U.S. policy. By 2002, Cheney and Wolfowitz, dominating the Pentagon, which in turn dominated the Bush administration, were setting U.S. policy, while their former colleagues James Baker and Lawrence Eagleburger, who had thwarted them between 1988 and 1992, could do no more than write op-eds and make TV appearances urging their employer's son, President George W. Bush, to pay attention to allies and international organizations. The revenge of the neoconservatives was complete.

The three pillars of the Wolfowitz–Bush Doctrine were American unilateralism, pre-emptive war, and the alignment of American foreign policy with that of Israel's right-wing leader Ariel Sharon. Each of these elements of George W. Bush's grand strategy represented a dramatic break with previous American foreign policy.

In its aggressive unilateralism, George W. Bush's presidency broke with a bipartisan tradition dating back to the end of World War II. Had its leaders wanted to do so, the United States in 1945 could have created a unilateral Pax Americana, along the lines of the defunct Pax Britannica. Instead, they chose to create a system of international institutions like the United Nations and NATO, in which the United States would lead by consensus rather than impose its will by force. During the Cold War, Soviet (and later communist Chinese) obstructionism prevented the Security Council from functioning as a great-power global steering committee. With the end of the Cold War, however, the UN began to function as its planners had intended—authorizing the Gulf War during the administration of the first Bush and the NATO intervention in the Balkans during the Clinton administration. Despite tactical disagreements, both George Herbert Walker Bush and Bill Clinton envisioned the "new world order" of which the first spoke as an extension of the existing UN/NATO system to new members and its adaptation to new needs.

George W. Bush, on assuming office in 2001, broke with the grand strategy of his father, as well as of his father's successor, Bill Clinton, and indeed with the grand strategy that had been followed, with minor differences in detail, by every American president since FDR. In his first year, Bush canceled more international treaties than any president in American history. The Kyoto Protocol on Global Warming, the Anti-Ballistic Missile Treaty, the small arms treaty, the International Criminal Court—these and other treaties, in force or negotiated, were abruptly canceled, leaving America's treaty partners insulted and shocked. In some cases, the treaties were arguably bad—the Kyoto Protocol needed to be amended, and the United States had legitimate concerns about politically motivated prosecutions of American soldiers and diplomats by the International Criminal Court. But the hostility of the second Bush administration toward treaties in general, as constraints on America's ability to act in a unilateral fashion, showed the influence of ideological dogmatism.

Wolfowitz and his allies argued that the unprecedented power of the United States, following the collapse of the Soviet Union, made a policy of unilateral American world domination unavoidable as well as desirable. But the United States in the early 2000s, with a GDP of no more than 20 percent of the world total, had far less relative power than it had in 1945, when the United States accounted for half of all industrial production in a war-devastated world. The greater relative power of the United States in 1945 did not prevent it from setting up a system of international institutions or working through alliances.

Another argument for unilateralism made by the Wolfowitzian neoconservatives invoked allegedly unprecedented threats of weapons of mass destruction and terrorism. But terrorism, often sponsored by the Soviet Union, had been a constant factor during the Cold War, and the Soviet nuclear, biological, and chemical arsenal had been a far greater threat to the United States and its allies than the relatively minor arsenals of Iraq, North Korea, and similar weak and bankrupt regimes. During the half-century Cold War, the United States defended itself from nuclear threats and terrorism in large part by means of the very international institutions and alliances that the neo-conservatives treated with contempt.

The announced adoption of pre-emptive warfare as a tactic by the administration of George W. Bush, like global unilateralism, was a break with both American and international traditions. During the Cuban Missile Crisis, when a pre-emptive U.S. attack on Soviet missiles in Cuba was being debated by President Kennedy's top advisers, Attorney General Robert F. Kennedy ended the debate by calling the proposal "Pearl Harbor in reverse" and declared, "For 175 years we have not been that kind of country." The Kennedy administration chose a blockade rather than a pre-emptive attack of the kind that Franklin Roosevelt attempted to stigmatize when he described December 7, 1941, as "a date which will live in infamy."

On June 7, 1981, Israeli F-16s flew into Iraqi territory and bombed Iraq's nuclear reactor at Osirak. The reaction of the international community was swift. The United States, which usually protects Israel from international condemnation, joined the UN Security Council in a unanimous resolution denouncing the Osirak raid. President

Ronald Reagan's ambassador to the United Nations, Jeane Kirk-patrick, compared the Israeli raid to the Soviet invasion of Afghani-stan, while the conservative Prime Minister of Britain, Margaret Thatcher, declared: "Armed attack in such circumstances cannot be justified. It represents a grave breach of international law."[7] The United States and its major allies agreed that war based on the mere suspicion that a rival state is developing weapons of mass destruction was unethical and illegal. Although the Reagan administration joined the other members of the UN Security Council in condemning Israel's raid on Iraq's Osirak reactor in 1981, American neoconservatives for the next two decades discussed the Osirak raid as a model of resource-ful statesmanship.

George W. Bush's departure from American foreign policy tradi-tion was equally striking in the case of U.S. policy toward Israel itself. Since the establishment of the state of Israel in 1948, every U.S. pres-ident, including those who were the most friendly to Israel, recognized the occasional divergence of interests between the two states. In 1957, Dwight Eisenhower thwarted Israel when it joined Britain and France in seizing the Suez Canal. During the 1967 war, Lyndon John-son, a longtime supporter of Israel, angered many American Jews when he took diplomatic objectives in the Middle East and the Cold War into account in ruling out direct U.S. intervention on Israel's behalf. Nixon aided Israel during the 1973 war, but he was a cold-blooded practitioner of domestic as well as international Realpolitik. Jimmy Carter began a modern tradition in which U.S. presidents attempted to act as "honest brokers" between Israel and its Arab neighbors, although the influence of the powerful Israel lobby in Washington, coupled with American sympathy for the only Western-style society in the Middle East, meant that most American attempts at mediation were biased to some degree. In 1981, Reagan arranged a cease-fire between Israel and the PLO and prevented Ariel Sharon from occupying Beirut during the Israeli invasion of Lebanon. Fol-lowing the Gulf War, George H. W. Bush fulfilled a promise to Amer-ica's Arab allies and pressured Israeli Prime Minister Yitzhak Shamir into attending the Madrid Conference. Bill Clinton supported the Oslo peace negotiations and hosted Rabin and Arafat at Camp David.

The offer that Rabin and Clinton made to Arafat—a Palestinian "state" that was nothing more than a series of discontiguous *bantustans,* or ethnic ghettoes—was unacceptable. But at Taba, Egypt, in December 2000, Israel and the Palestinians came close to agreeing on a different plan acceptable in its broad outlines to moderates on both sides.

Then the Labour Prime Minister Ehud Barak was defeated and replaced by Ariel Sharon, one of the most grim warriors of Israel's far-right Likud Party. Sharon's provocative visit to the al-Aksa Mosque—which Jewish religious fanatics in Israel and the United States want to demolish and replace with a "third temple"—provoked the second intifada, or Palestinian uprising. During his first year in office, Bush minimized U.S. involvement in the Middle East crisis, which escalated as Sharon used increasing Palestinian attacks on Israeli forces and citizens to carry out a long-cherished Likud dream of abandoning the Oslo peace process and reoccupying the West Bank. Instead, the Bush administration, after a period of ambiguity between September 2001 and June 2002, in which Colin Powell's State Department was defeated and humiliated by pro-Israel hawks in the Defense Department, adopted as American policy what the far right wing in Israeli politics had been advocating for a decade: a refusal to negotiate with the Palestinian Authority and its elected leader, Yasser Arafat, and insistence on the development of full-scale democracy in Palestine, of a kind that existed nowhere else in the region, as a precondition for an end to Israel's brutal thirty-five-year-occupation of the territory belonging to three million Palestinians. The policies of the Bush administration were presented as a response to the violence committed by Palestinian suicide bombers and a plausible road map to a Palestinian state within three years, but in reality they were merely the endorsement, by the U.S. government, of Israeli delaying tactics that would allow Israel to reoccupy the West Bank and expand its settlements for another ten or twenty years.

The Bush–Wolfowitz plan for American foreign policy was opposed by the mainstream U.S. foreign policy elite and by a majority of the

American people, who according to polls opposed U.S. military action in Iraq and elsewhere without the support of allies and international institutions like the United Nations. The foreign policy of the radical right was enthusiastically supported by only two groups in the United States—neoconservative policymakers and intellectuals at the elite level, and Southern Protestant voters within the mass voting public.

Neoconservatives were not traditional conservative Republicans. Most had been liberal or leftist Democrats; some had originally been Marxists. Many were Jewish and had broken with the Democratic left because of leftist hostility to Israel's occupation of Arab land after 1967 and the hostility of many Black Power militants to both Jewish-Americans and Israel. Ronald Reagan was the first Republican president that many neoconservatives had voted for. While the foreign policy of the traditional Republican establishment reflected the fear of international disorder of the business elite, neoconservative strategy reflected the crusading ideological fervor of former Wilsonian liberals and former Marxist revolutionaries, combined, in the case of many Jewish neoconservatives, with an emotional ethnic commitment to the well-being of Israel.

"You hear from some of Wolfowitz's critics, always off the record, that Israel exercises a powerful gravitational pull on the man," the journalist Bill Keller wrote in the *New York Times Magazine* on September 22, 2002. "They may not know that as a teenager he spent his father's sabbatical semester in Israel or that his sister is married to an Israeli, but they certainly know that he is friendly with Israel's generals and diplomats and that he is something of a hero to the heavily Jewish neoconservative movement."[8] Throughout the second Bush administration, Wolfowitz, the second most powerful figure at the Pentagon, acted openly and unapologetically as a liaison between the executive branch and pro-Israel Jewish institutions like the America Israel Public Affairs Committee (AIPAC). At a pro-Israel rally in Washington, D.C., attended not only by Jews but by right-wing Protestant fundamentalists, Wolfowitz represented the Bush administration. Even Wolfowitz was not hawkish enough for the Jewish and Christian Zionists in the crowd, who booed him when he said a few perfunctory lines about the suffering of the Palestinians. In an address to the American Jewish Committee on May 4, 2001, he said, "When Saddam Hussein was launching terror weapons called SCUDs against Israel, I was there with Deputy Secretary of State Lawrence Eagleburger. We saw children walking to school carrying gas masks in gaily decorated boxes—no doubt to try to distract them from the possibility of facing mass destruction."[9] Wolfowitz told the American Jewish Committee that Iraq and other "irresponsible powers"—presumably Iran and Syria—"are already within missile range of Israel and our other allies in the region."[10] (Israel, in violation of international treaties and norms, reportedly possesses hundreds of nuclear weapons, as well as unknown quantities of chemical and biological weapons, but mention of this fact remains taboo in the American press and American politics.)

Just as troubling was the close relationship between Ariel Sharon's Likud Party and Richard Perle, the head of Bush's Defense Policy Board, an influential advisory panel of outside experts. Perle, based at the conservative American Enterprise Institute in Washington, heads Hollinger Digital, part of the Hollinger media empire run by the British tycoon Conrad Black, owner of the right-wing *Jerusalem Post,* whose board meetings Perle attended. Another leader of the Wolfowitz faction in the Bush administration was Douglas J. Feith, a Washington attorney with extensive business dealings in Israel. In 1996, Perle, Feith, and others were commissioned to co-author a paper for the Likud Prime Minister Benjamin Netanyahu. Entitled "A Clean Break: A New Strategy for Securing the Realm," Perle and Feith advised the Israelis to make "a clean break from the peace process." A year later, in an essay entitled "A Strategy for Israel," Feith proposed that Israel reoccupy "the areas under Palestinian Authority control" even though "the price in blood would be high." Earlier in 1993, in the foreign policy quarterly *The National Interest,* Feith had made a specious argument that the League of Nations mandate granted Jews irrevocable settlement rights in the West Bank. On October 13, 1997, Feith and his father were given awards by the right-wing Zionist Organization of America, which described the honorees only as "the noted Jewish philanthropists and pro-Israel activists." Douglas Feith, appointed as undersecretary of defense for policy, became the third most important policymaker in the Defense Department of George W.

Bush. After Perle and Feith joined the Bush administration, Israel's Ariel Sharon, with the support of the U.S. government, carried out the policy of repudiating the Oslo peace process and reoccupying the West Bank—and "the price in blood" was indeed high.[11]

The disturbing links between the Israeli right and the neoconservatives in the executive branch were not limited to Jewish-American officials. Dick Cheney and John Bolton were affiliated with the Jewish Institute for National Security Affairs (JINSA), a lobby group in Washington that spent millions of dollars disseminating the views of the far right in Israel. For many non-Jewish neoconservatives, as well as their Jewish allies, Israel had long ago replaced Britain as America's major partner in world politics. Former secretary of education and drug czar William Bennett, a Catholic neoconservative, even suggested that the United States and Israel, alone among the nations of the world, shared a mission from God: "I myself am one of tens of millions of Americans who have seen in the founding and flourishing of the Jewish state the hand of the same beneficent God who attended our own founding and has guided our fortunes until now."[12]

In the aftermath of the al-Qaeda attacks, several eminent neoconservatives spontaneously declared, "We are all Israelis now." What seemed to be a metaphor now looks like a program for American foreign policy. Under George W. Bush, the American executive branch and the government of Israel were fused in a degree without precedent in American history. Even in the days of Anglo-American cooperation during World War II, the United States and Britain often fought bitterly, and Anglophiles never dominated the domestic political debate the way that the Israel lobby intimidated dissenters in Congress and the major U.S. media outlets. Indeed, some career officials in the U.S. executive branch privately described the grand strategy of George W. Bush as "the Israelization of American foreign policy." In the Israeli-Palestinian conflict, the Bush administration has sided with Ariel Sharon, to the extent of treating Yasser Arafat, the legitimately elected president of Palestine, as a mere criminal whom the United States refuses to deal with. The Project for the New American Century, a neoconservative think tank that disseminated the thinking of the Wolfowitz circle, called on the U.S. military not only to eliminate Saddam Hussein's regime in Iraq but also to threaten or engage in pre-emptive U.S. military strikes against Iran, Syria, Hezbollah, and other states and militant groups that shared nothing in common other than opposition to the state of Israel.[13] In attacking Israel's enemies, the United States, according to the neoconservatives, should adopt the tactic of unprovoked pre-emptive war that Israel used when it attacked Iraq in the Osirak raid of June 7, 1981. In its new unilateralism in global affairs, the United States would adopt the contemptuous attitude toward the United Nations and international law that Israel has shown following its occupation of the Palestinian territories in 1967—a stance not incompatible with occasional strong-arming of the UN Security Council by Washington in the service of American and Israeli goals. Bizarre as it seems, thanks to the influence of the Israeli model on neoconservatives in the Bush administration, the United States, the leading power in the world, began acting as though it were an insecure and besieged international pariah state, like Israel under the leadership of the Likud Party.

The Jewish hawks in the Bush administration and their journalistic allies like William Kristol, Charles Krauthammer, and William Safire were not representative of Jewish-Americans in general. Most Jewish voters in 2000 preferred Al Gore to George W. Bush. A Gore administration, while solicitous of Israeli interests, would not have given Ariel Sharon permission to destroy the basis for Palestinian statehood, made an American invasion and occupation of Iraq its central priority, or adopted a radical policy of Israeli-style unilateralism instead of building on the post–Cold War internationalism of both George Herbert Walker Bush and Bill Clinton. The faction of Jewish and non-Jewish neoconservatives within the Republican Party would have had little or no influence on American foreign policy, if not for its tactical alliance with the voters who secured the Republican presidential nomination for George W. Bush, the voters whose zeal he needs to be reelected: white Southern Protestants. The strategic brains for George W. Bush's foreign policy were provided by neoconservatives like Paul Wolfowitz, but the Deep South provided the political muscle.

The unilateral imperialism of the neoconservatives, like their pro-Israel and anti-Iraq policies, was reinforced in national politics by the centuries-old political culture of conservative white voters in the American South. In the case of the Bush administration's withdrawal of the United States from a treaty to prevent the proliferation of small arms, arguing that it might infringe on the constitutional right of Americans to own guns, the influence of the gun-owning culture of the South and parts of the Mountain West on American unilateralism is obvious. More important, however, is a tradition of hostility toward diplomacy and international organizations rooted in both Southern militarism and Southern religious fundamentalism.

White Southerners are not isolationists or pacifists. On the contrary, from the eighteenth century until the present, they have been more eager than white Northerners to support American wars abroad. According to the historian David Hackett Fischer, "From the quasi-war with France [in 1798] to the Vietnam War, the two southern cultures strongly supported every American war no matter what it was about or who it was against. Southern ideas of honor and the warrior ethic combined to create regional war fevers of great intensity in 1798, 1812, 1846, 1861, 1898, 1917, 1941, 1950 and 1965."[14] In an August 2002 Gallup poll, 24 percent of Southerners agreed with the statement: "The United States should send troops even if none of our Western allies supports that action." Only 15 percent of Midwesterners agreed. While Midwesterners were almost evenly divided—47 percent in favor and 44 percent against—Southerners favored an invasion of Iraq by 62 percent to 34 percent.[15] One journalist described the constituency with the most fervent support for Bush's proposed war against Iraq: "If you put these different proportions together, you get a high-school-educated white male from the rural or small-town South."[16] When the House of Representatives voted on October 10, 2002, to authorize George W. Bush to go to war with Iraq, a majority of Democrats voted against the resolution. Most of the Democrats who broke with their party to support Bush were from Southern states like Texas, Alabama, Arkansas, Florida, Kentucky, Louisiana, and

Mississippi; the entire Democratic delegation of Tennessee joined all of their Republican colleagues in voting for war.[17] With considerable reason, then, in a memoir entitled *White Southern Warrior*, Joseph Marvin writes: "Since 1865, national American leaders only like us white southrons when they want to go to war."[18]

The support of white Southerners for military intervention abroad is not to be confused with internationalism. Rather, it takes the form of unilateral militarism, which is compatible with a contempt for civilian diplomacy. In *Dixie Looks Abroad: The South and U.S. Foreign Relations, 1789–1973* (2002), the historian Joseph A. Fry observes: "While adopting the stance of cold warriors, the vast majority of southerners cast aside any pretense of internationalism. The South quickly became disillusioned with the United Nations after 1945 and persistently favored unilateral actions when U.S. interests were in question."[19] From the earliest days of the American Republic, white Southerners have been represented above their proportion of the U.S. population in the armed forces—and greatly under-represented among members of the Foreign Service, which until recently was a bastion of patrician Northeasterners. The Mason-Dixon line might as well run through the Potomac River between the Pentagon and the State Department.

Throughout the twentieth century, many white Southerners were hostile to the League of Nations, the United Nations, and other international organizations, for two reasons—one racial, one religious. The racial reason, important in the decades before the Civil Rights Revolution, was the fear that international human rights treaties might be interpreted to require the abolition of racial segregation in the South. While the civil rights reforms of the 1960s eliminated the rationale for this kind of rejectionism, the legacy persisted in the efforts of North Carolina Senator Jesse Helms for decades afterward to prevent the ratification by the Senate of various international human rights covenants.

More important than vestigial racism today is the religious motive for hostility to international organization: the sincere belief on the part of many Southern Protestant fundamentalists that the United Nations, the European Union, or some other international organization or multinational bloc is under the control of Satan. Most Americans, as well as most foreigners, find it difficult to believe that anyone in an advanced industrial society can believe this. But millions of Americans, particularly in the Deep South, have grown up listening to local pastors or television or radio preachers explain that the European Union is one of the horns of the multiple-headed dragon of the Book of Revelation, or that the UN is the "Beast" described in the same book.

The fact that many members of the religious-right base of the Republican Party believe in this apocalyptic ideology endows many statements by conservative politicians like George W. Bush with a double meaning—one for the general public, one for the conservative base. When, during his campaign, he argued against using American peace-keeping troops on UN missions in places like Bosnia, most Americans assumed that this reflected a distinct but reasonable Republican military doctrine. Indeed, there are legitimate secular reasons for Bush's approach, and valid arguments could be made for the Bush administration's threat to withdraw U.S. troops from UN peace-keeping in the Balkans unless American soldiers were exempted from prosecution by the new, Europe-based International Criminal Court (ICC).

But words and actions that have one meaning to the international diplomatic elite have another in Mississippi, Virginia—and Texas. In 1995, Michael New, a soldier from Texas in the U.S. Army assigned to peace-keeping duty in the Balkans, refused to put on a UN beret. Court-martialed, he became a folk hero to the far right in his native Texas and the United States. His father, from his home in Texas, established a web site on his behalf, in which the alleged UN plan for world government is explained.[20] To dismiss Americans like New and his supporters as members of the lunatic fringe was mistaken. They were the political base of the Bush administration and the contemporary, Southernized Republican Party. According to polls, the groups that showed least support for U.S. participation in UN peace-keeping efforts in Kosovo were Southerners and those without college degrees.[21]

It is a mistake, then, to attribute the radical unilateralism of George W. Bush's presidency solely to new global conditions or the theories of this or that neoconservative policymaker or intellectual.

The fact that the United States, after the Cold War, was the only global superpower did not make the adoption of Bush-style unilateralism either necessary or desirable. After all, the United States after 1945 was far more powerful relative to the other great powers than it was after 1989—and yet the mid-century United States, accounting for half of the industrial production and most of the military power on the planet, used its wealth and power to create a system of international institutions that the Bush administration, leading a relatively weaker United States, set about consciously to dismantle.

Nor should the influence of neoconservative intellectuals on conservative unilateralism be exaggerated. As we have seen, the most influential strategic thinker in the second Bush administration was Paul Wolfowitz, who argued that the United States should engage in a vast military buildup to maintain its military superiority over all powers indefinitely. But Wolfowitz had made the same argument in the Pentagon policy planning paper in 1992, when he had served in the administration of the first Bush. The argument was no more compelling in 2001 and 2002 than it had been in 1992. The difference in Wolfowitz's influence in the two Bush administrations reflected the increasing importance of the South in the Republican Party, as well as a very real difference between the soft-spoken, diplomacy-minded Northeastern internationalist father and the macho, swaggering, Southern born-again Protestant son, a genuine cultural Texan.

The Wolfowitz–Bush doctrine of unilateral militarism, influenced by the unilateralism of the Israeli government, was easily identified with the preferred foreign policy tradition of the American South, dating back to the earliest years of the Republic. The noted historian and political analyst Walter Russell Mead has called this tradition "Jacksonianism."[22] If it seems bizarre to both establishment conservatives and mainstream liberals, it is only because no Southern conservative had been elected to the White House between the pre–Civil War era and 2000.

The martial tradition of the American South, rooted in the ethos of the British aristocracy that colonial-era "cavaliers" transplanted to the

American South, is shared broadly by white Southerners, including many who are secular and progressive. In contrast, the alignment of the foreign policies of George W. Bush's America and Ariel Sharon's Israel reflects the influence of a particular subculture in the South: Protestant fundamentalists.

The figure with the greatest influence on the Middle Eastern policy of George W. Bush, at the level of mass electoral politics rather than elite policymaking, is a long-dead English preacher, John Nelson Darby (1800–1882). It is unlikely that Bush, born-again Christian though he is, has ever heard of Darby. But the Protestant tradition that Darby founded has had a profound influence on the politics of the American South and, through George W. Bush, on American foreign policy.

John Nelson Darby was an Anglican priest in Ireland who abandoned the Church of England in the 1820s and founded his own sect, the Brethren, which spread throughout the British Isles, Germany, North America, and elsewhere. Over many years Darby worked out the elaborate theory of premillennial dispensationalism, which influences American Protestant fundamentalist belief today. Darby's vision of history, scarcely altered by his successors, holds that in the "end times" Israel will be re-created as a nation-state. God will intervene repeatedly to save Israel. Eventually, however, the state of Israel will be destroyed in the battle of Armageddon, in which an international confederation—perhaps the United Nations, perhaps the European Union—will be led by the Antichrist, whom many fundamentalists believe will be an apostate Jew. Most Jews will be killed, but 144,000 will convert to Christianity. Jesus will physically return to earth in order to defeat the Antichrist. At that point, the Jewish Temple on the Temple Mount (where al-Aksa Mosque stands today) will be restored, along with the throne of King David. Having returned to earth, Jesus will establish a world government in the form of a theocracy and rule as a benevolent dictator for the next thousand years, whereupon Satan will escape, only to be defeated once again—this time forever.

The first major American evangelical Protestants to adopt Darbyism were Dwight L. Moody, founder of the Moody Bible Institute of Chicago, and Cyrus Scofield of the Dallas Theological Seminary, whose *Scofield Reference Bible* has persuaded generations of Protestant fundamentalists in the United States and abroad that Darby's bizarre interpretation of Scripture is the authentic one. A graduate of that Dallas school, Hal Lindsey spread the Darby–Scofield theory of history in a number of apocalyptic best-sellers, including *The Late, Great Planet Earth*. The premillennialist dispensationalism of John Nelson Darby has led American Protestant fundamentalists to view the foundation of the state of Israel as a sign that the end of history was approaching. The victory of Israel in 1967, and its conquest and occupation of the West Bank and the Gaza Strip, created a wave of apocalyptic enthusiasm among Protestant fundamentalists in the United States, particularly in Texas and other Southern states. The restoration of Jews to all of the Holy Land became a priority for the Southern right a generation before the Southern right hijacked the national Republican Party.

While their vision of the future obviously differs, the Protestant Zionists along with Jewish religious Zionists cite passages like God's promise to Abraham in Genesis 15:18: "To your descendants I give this land, from the river of Egypt to the great river, the Euphrates." By 2002, Protestant fundamentalists in the United States had launched an "adopt-a-settlement" program. Texan fundamentalists played a leading role. In 1998, John Hagee, pastor of the Cornerstone Church in San Antonio, Texas, announced that the congregation would give more than $1 million to the government of Israel to resettle Jews from the former Soviet Union in the West Bank and Jerusalem. To the observation that according to U.S. law the Jewish settlements in the West Bank were illegal, Hagee replied: "I am a Bible scholar and theologian and from my perspective, the law of God transcends the law of the United States government and the U.S. State Department." According to Hagee, the Israeli colonization of land stolen from its Arab inhabitants in the West Bank and Gaza Strip "is a fulfillment of biblical prophecy."[23] Some American fundamentalists are allied with Jewish religious fanatics who dream of destroying the al-Aqsa Mosque in order to build a "Third Temple" on the Temple Mount.

The leading conservative members of Congress from Texas were among the most fervent supporters of the far right in Israel. In the last week of April 2002, House Majority Whip Tom DeLay said that all of the West Bank—which he followed the practice of the Jewish and Christian religious right in calling "Judea and Samaria"—belonged to Israel, presumably because God gave it to Abraham and his descendants. On May 1, 2002, on MSNBC's program "Hardball," House Republican Majority Leader Armey endorsed the call of the Israeli right for the ethnic cleansing by Israeli military of the West Bank and Gaza of native Palestinians. "I'm content to have Israel grab the entire West Bank." When Chris Matthews, the host, replied, "Well, where do you put the Palestinian state, in Norway?" Armey answered, "I happen to believe the Palestinians should leave." Stunned, Matthews said, "Well, just to repeat, you believe that the Palestinians who are now living on the West Bank should get out of there?" Armey replied, "Yes." The congressman from Texas proposed that the Israeli military expel more than three million people from their homeland—a war crime comparable to the attempted ethnic cleansing by Serbian nationalists of the Muslim majority of Kosovo that the United States and its NATO allies had gone to war a few years earlier to prevent.

As early as the 1960s, one Texan fundamentalist, convinced that the establishment of the state of Israel proved that the end of the world was near, had journeyed to Israel and established a small group of believers in that country. His name was George Roden, and he was the leader of a congregation in Waco, Texas, to which, inspired by the traditions of ancient Israel, he had given the name Branch Davidians.

The fervent support of Israel by Protestant fundamentalists, rooted in John Nelson Darby's idiosyncratic interpretation of the Bible, has been manipulated for a quarter of a century by right-wing Israeli politicians and their American neoconservative allies.

From 1948 until 1977, the dominant Labour Party kept the authoritarian racial and religious nationalists of the Likud Party and its allies out of power. Menachem Begin was the first Likud prime minister, followed by Yitzhak Shamir, Benjamin Netanyahu, and Ariel Sharon. The Likud Party opposed the Oslo peace agreements, and Likud Prime Minister Netanyahu did his best to undermine them. It was Ariel Sharon who abandoned the Oslo process altogether and, with the Bush administration's approval, destroyed the infrastructure of the Palestinian authority, assassinated or arrested both militant and moderate PLO leaders, and prevailed on Bush to break off all contacts with the elected president, Yasser Arafat. Inspired by the racial nationalism of Zeev (Vladimir) Jabotinsky (1880–1940), a right-wing Zionist who modeled his Revisionist Zionist movement on Mussolini's fascism, down to the brown shirts worn by his Jewish terrorist squads, the majority of the Likud Party and its allies wanted Israel to annex permanently all of the land west of Jordan. The major debate among Likudniks was whether to "transfer" three million Arabs in an act of wholesale ethnic cleansing, or to rule the Arabs indefinitely, converting Israel into an apartheid state in which the Arabs would have no political rights and would work as menial laborers for Jewish colonists in conditions of racial segregation.

In 1967, the Israelis were praised by the right-wing Hearst media empire, a precursor of the late-twentieth-century Murdoch empire in its combination of sensational tabloid journalism and conservative politics. The John Birch Society gave $300,000 to the United Jewish Appeal.[24] But these anti-communist conservatives, who viewed Israel as a bulwark against the expansion of Soviet influence in the Arab world, were less important in the long run than the Protestant fundamentalists who interpreted the Israeli victory as a sign that biblical prophecies about the end of the world had been confirmed.

When Menachem Begin came to power in 1977, Donald Wagner writes, "Likud's strategy was simple: split evangelical and fundamentalist Christians from Carter's political base and rally support among conservative Christians for Israel's opposition to the United Nations' proposed Middle East Peace Conference."[25] Since then, Protestant fundamentalists have acted as an echo chamber for the Israeli Likud Party: supporting Israel's invasion of Lebanon in 1982, opposing the Oslo peace process, demanding an end to U.S. negotiations with Palestinians, and encouraging the expansion of Jewish settlements in "Eretz Israel."

The Likud Party's most important lobbyist in the United States may have been Jerry Falwell, the Baptist preacher in Lynchburg, Viriginia, who founded the Moral Majority. In 1981, after Israel bombed Iraq's nuclear facility in Osirak, Begin phoned Jerry Falwell before he spoke to President Reagan (who condemned the Israeli raid). Begin asked Falwell to "explain to the Christian public the reasons for the bombing."[26] In 1979, the government of Israel gave Falwell his own Lear jet.[27] In 1998, when Benjamin Netanyahu visited Washington, D.C., before he met with President Clinton he addressed more than a thousand Protestant fundamentalists, including Jerry Falwell. The fundamentalists promised to mobilize to "tell President Clinton to refrain from putting pressure on Israel" to carry out its agreements under the Oslo accords.[28]

Most American Jews were frightened by the religious right, many of whose leaders made anti-semitic statements. Bailey Smith, a Dallas pastor, declared that "God does not hear the prayer of a Jew," and Pat Robertson, in his book *The New World Order,* claimed that Jewish financiers along with Freemasons and satanists had caused the French Revolution and many of the major wars of the past two hundred years.[29] Timothy Weber, dean of the Northern Baptist Theological Seminary in Chicago, explains that American fundamentalists "find it easy to appreciate Jews for prophetic reasons, especially those in Israel, but they have very negative feelings about other Jews who may be to the left politically or theologically, and they're able to keep those two diametrically opposed feelings quite separate and not worry about it."[30]

Billy Graham, the revivalist who converted George W. Bush in his late 30s to evangelical Protestant fundamentalism, is an example. Like many Protestant fundamentalists, Graham combined hostility to liberal Jewish-Americans with a theologically mandated respect for Israeli Jews. Graham explained to Nixon and his aides that "a lot of the Jews are great friends of mine. They swarm around me and are friendly to me. Because they know I am friendly to Israel and so forth. They don't know how I really feel about what they're doing to this country."[31] The historian of religion Martin E. Marty observes: "Billy Graham's taped words to President Nixon reinforce the idea that evangelicals were often domestically (culturally more than theologically) 'anti-Semitic' but theologically and politically 'pro-Zionist.'"[32]

This distinction was emphasized by opportunistic cynics on the Jewish right. In 1995, after I exposed the anti-semitic sources of Pat Robertson's theories about a two-century-old Judeo-Masonic conspiracy in a widely read essay in the *New York Review of Books,* Norman Podhoretz, the editor of *Commentary,* conceded that Robertson's statements about Jews were objectively anti-semitic but argued that, in light of Robertson's support for Israel, he should be excused according to the ancient rabbinical rule of *batel b'shishim*: "if the contaminant has slipped in accidentally or unintentionally, and is no more than one-sixtieth of the whole, it is neutralized and the food can be lawfully eaten."[33] If he cooperates with the Israel lobby, even a Jew-baiting Protestant preacher can be certified as kosher. The opportunistic approach of most Jewish neoconservatives toward Southern fundamentalists was summed up by Irving Kristol in 1984 in *Commentary,* the magazine of the American Jewish Committee: "Why should Jews care about the theology of a fundamentalist preacher? . . . What do such theological abstractions matter as against the mundane fact that this same preacher is vigorously pro-Israel?"[34] The alliance of the religious right and the neoconservatives was cemented in 1981, when the government of Israel gave the Reverend Jerry Falwell the Jabotinsky Award. Two decades later, in 2002, the Zionist Organization of America—which a few years earlier had honored Douglas Feith, the third most powerful policymaker in George W. Bush's Defense Department, as a "pro-Israel activist"—gave an award to Pat Robertson for his services to Israel.

The need to enlist Southern Protestant fundamentalists as allies explains troubling inconsistencies in the neoconservative conception of American patriotism. On August 26, 2000, editor William Kristol of *The Weekly Standard* denounced "an axis of appeasement—stretching from Riyadh to Brussels to Foggy Bottom, from Howell Raines to Chuck Hagel to Brent Scowcroft."[35] While the neoconservatives denounced Republican Senator Chuck Hagel (a Vietnam combat veteran) and former National Security Adviser Brent Scowcroft, a career military officer, as "appeasers," they avoided bitter denunciations of pro-Israel fundamentalists, even when they made unpatriotic statements.

On September 13, 2001, on Pat Robertson's television show *The 700 Club,* Jerry Falwell attributed the terrorist attacks on the previous Tuesday to God: "God continues to lift the curtain and allow the enemies of America to give us probably what we deserve." As Robertson, the founder of the Christian Coalition, expressed his agreement, Falwell blamed the attack on federal judges and "the pagans and the abortionists and the feminists and the gays and the lesbians . . . the ACLU, People for the American Way. . . . I point the finger in their face and say, 'You helped this happen.'" The suicidal terrorists who flew hijacked planes into the World Trade Center, the Pentagon, and the ground in Pennsylvania believed that they were on a mission from God. Jerry Falwell and Pat Robertson agreed.

Were the two preachers ostracized by the rest of the American right for their shocking comments? Were they denounced as traitors or—to use the favorite word of the neoconservative, "appeasers"? A White House spokesman politely regretted Falwell's language—but he was a guest of honor at the National Cathedral service commemorating the September 11 events. Robertson, whose fundamentalist followers had won the Republican presidential nomination for George Bush, suffered no diminution of influence in the party. A few neoconservative editors mildly reprimanded and then forgave Falwell and Robertson. Experienced combat veterans who raised practical questions about the feasibility of the neoconservative plan for an American occupation of Iraq and an Israeli-American condominium in the Middle East were vilified as "appeasers," if not traitors, while neoconservatives said little or nothing about the Southern fundamentalist preachers who said that the 3,000 Americans and resident foreigners murdered on September 11, 2001, were legitimate victims of God's punishment of American society. The preachers may have been unpatriotic and anti-American, but they were, in the words of Irving Kristol, "vigorously pro-Israel."

The idea that Osama bin Laden was simply God's instrument for punishing a faithless America showed signs of becoming a new orthodoxy among the core supporters of George W. Bush. On Friday, October 11, 2002, little more than a year after the terrorist attacks, Joyce Meyer of Joyce Meyer Ministries of Fenton, Missouri, told the Christian Coalition's annual "Road to Victory" Conference that the American people deserved to be attacked. "If we don't obey God, God's protection is lifted," Meyer explained. On the same day, President Bush greeted the delegates with a video message, in which he promised to continue promoting the agenda of the religious right.[36]

The alliance of the white Southern Protestant fundamentalists and Jewish neoconservatives was strengthened by a sense that they were embattled and despised minorities not only in the world but in their own ethnic groups. The Jewish right was a minority within the American Jewish community, which remained predominantly liberal in domestic policy, and the Southern right had always been a minority among white Americans.

A sense of a peoplehood distinct from that felt by Americans as a whole was also shared by conservative Jews and many conservative white Southerners. Explanations of the affinity between the Southern right and the Israeli Jewish right in terms of a supposed affinity between two "democracies," the United States and Israel, like the supposed tradition of amity between the "revolutionary republics" of the United States and France, were misleading propaganda. Enlightenment ideals of liberal democracy had nothing to do with the mutual admiration society between Jewish settlers on Arab land and Anglo-Scots-Irish settlers on American Indian and Mexican land. The affinity was that of one ethnoreligious tribalism for another. Yehoshua Arieli, a liberal Israeli scholar, wrote in 1964 that American patriotism is founded on abstract principles: "The American people were not a folk-nation or a federation of nations. They lacked ethnic, religious, or cultural unity, and all those traits which a common history impressed upon territorial societies."[37] Whether or not this had ever been true of mainstream American nationalism, it was not true of the identity politics of the white South, even in the twenty-first century. The Anglo-Celtic Protestants of the American South are a "folk-nation." They have "ethnic" unity; most are descendants of English, Scottish, Scots-Irish, or Welsh immigrants. They have "religious" unity; almost all are evangelical Protestants of one denomination or another. They have "cultural" unity, sharing a common set of folkways and accents that defined the section from Texas to Virginia and the Florida panhandle as a nation-within-the-nation. And they have "a common history" impressed on their "territorial" society. Few of them had ancestors who had immigrated to North America later than 1776; for many Southerners west of the Atlantic seaboard, the folk-memory of westward migration through the South and the service of family members in the Confederate Army is part of living tradition. White Southerners belong to a tribe—a tribe that has far more genuine unity, in every respect, than Israeli Jews from various traditions—Ashkenazic and Sephardic, Spanish and Russian and North African.

The fierce religiosity of Anglo-Celtic Texans, like so much else, can be traced back via Tennessee and West Virginia to Ulster and Scotland. The eighteenth-century Scots who moved to the American colonies from Northern Ireland combined frontier ferocity with simple and fervent Calvinist Protestantism. (Each man in the fabled Scottish Cameronian regiment in the British Army was equipped with a Bible and a dagger.) Like the Protestant Dutch Afrikaaners of South Africa, the Protestant Scots-Irish Southerners compared themselves to the ancient Hebrews. So, of course, did black Americans. But whereas black Americans dwelled on the Exodus of the Hebrews from slavery in Egypt, the Southerners much preferred the chapters in "the Bobble" about the conquest of the Promised Land and the genocide of the Canaanites. For all their nominal Christianity, white Southerners have never been comfortable with meek and mild Jesus, who turned himself over for execution without a fight and counseled his followers to turn the other cheek when struck and to forgive their enemies. Deep down, all true Southerners prefer Hebrew tribal generals like Moses, Joshua, Gideon, and David.

It is not for nothing that Southern religion has been called "Old Testament Protestantism." The Southern Protestant conception of morality resembles that of Orthodox Jews or traditional Muslims. It consists of strict obedience to God-given Old Testament law, which is thought to be less binding on Christians to this day. The laws governing morals in Texas and other Southern states are near-literal transcriptions from the Book of Leviticus. Protestant preachers mobilize their flocks to prevent the repeal of archaic sodomy laws, for fear that Dallas and Houston will be punished like Sodom and Gomorrah.

In addition to being legalistic, Old Testament Protestant morality is communal. A single moral code traditionally has been enforced by the community, employers, schools, the state, and—until a few decades ago—the lynch mob. Among clannish, tight-knit, old-fashioned Anglo-Celtic Protestant Southerners, as among Orthodox Jews, there is little toleration for individual deviance from tribal norms.

The gun-toting, Bible-thumping Anglo-Celtic Texan in former Mexican and Indian territories, with his admiration for the Hebrew patriarchs and professed devotion to the Ten Commandments, is remarkably similar to the gun-toting, Torah-thumping Israeli settler in the occupied Arab territories. The "sabra" ideal of a certain strain of Zionism—macho, militaristic, pious—is a cousin of the Southern/Western "redneck" or "cowboy," down to the contempt for the disposable "Canaanites"—blacks and Mexican-Americans in Texas and Arabs in Israel. Like present-day Israel, Texas before the Civil Rights Revolution was a *Herrenvolk* (master race) democracy, combining populism within the majority ethnic nation with the state-enforced subordination of ethnic minorities. It is no coincidence that the products of two similar *Herrenvolk* societies, George W. Bush and Ariel Sharon, appear to be most themselves when waging war on behalf of their tribes or relaxing on their ranches. Indeed, what the Scots-Irish did to the native Irish Catholics in the seventeenth century is remarkably similar to what the most militant Jewish colonists did to the native Arab Palestinians in the twentieth century. The historian George M. Fredrickson writes: "The late sixteenth- and early seventeenth century colonization projects [in Ireland] were accompanied by virtually every kind of atrocity that would ever be perpetrated against American Indians—women and children were massacred, captured rebels were executed, or enslaved, and whole communities were uprooted and consigned to special reservations. . . . Four fifths of the six counties of Northern Ireland were set aside for the exclusive occupancy of English or Scottish settlers; the native Irish were

either driven out of Ulster or concentrated in the residual one fifth—
a series of small reservations which they were forbidden to leave on
penalty of death."[38]

The parallels between whites in the historic black belt in the Deep
South and the Israeli-occupied territories in Palestine go further. In
each case, a minority surrounded by a repressed population without
rights lives in fear of rebellion by the subjugated majority. In each
case, the isolated minority promulgates an ideology of racial and religious solidarity to enlist the support of its ethnic kin in the area where
they are majority to help them rule the subjugated. The black belt produced one-party politics in the South; the occupation of the territory
of Arab populations has produced national-unity government in
Israel. After 1830, the defense of slavery and later segregation in the
Old South led white Southerners to abandon the enlightened liberal
idealism of the Founding era for harsh racism and a siege mentality.
Since 1967, the need to justify the rule of Israel over a conquered
helot population has produced a similar shift from humane idealism
to unapologetic tribalism in the Jewish diaspora as well as in Israel
proper.

With good reason, then, T. R. Fehrenbach, the Texan historian, a
generation ago compared the Anglo-Texans to the Israelis. The anal-
ogy occurred to an Israeli prime minister. During a speech in Dallas,
Texas on April 11, 2002, former Prime Minister Benjamin Netanyahu
shocked many in the audience by making a contemptuous compari-
son between Palestinian Arabs and Mexicans.[39]

––––––––––––––––––––

In his approach to the Middle East, the first President Bush and his
advisers like Secretary of State James Baker had reflected the pro-
Arab tilt of traditional business elites in the Texas oil patch, rescuing
Kuwait from Saddam Hussein while pressuring Israel to avoid retali-
ation against Iraqi attacks and to attend the Madrid peace conference
with its Arab neighbors following the Gulf War. In September 1991,
the first President Bush complained that "there are 1,000 lobbyists
up on the Hill today lobbying Congress for loan guarantees for Israel

and I'm one lonely little guy down here asking Congress to delay its consideration of loan guarantees for 120 days."

The wrath directed by the bipartisan Israel lobby against the elder Bush in the early 1990s was no doubt remembered by the son. And the prospect that a pro-Likud Israel policy would attract some Jewish donors, whose contributions were more important than the small number of Jewish votes, to the Republican Party no doubt appealed to some Republican strategists. But there is little doubt that the bonding between George W. Bush and Ariel Sharon was based on conviction, not expedience. Like the Christian Zionist base of the Republican Party, George W. Bush was a devout Southern fundamentalist.

In his campaign autobiography, *A Charge to Keep,* Bush describes his trip to Israel as part of a group of American politicians paid for by the National Jewish Coalition: "Our delegation included four gentile governors—one Methodist, two Catholics, and a Mormon, and several Jewish-American friends." Bush writes, "It was an overwhelming feeling to stand in the spot [at the Sea of Galilee] where the most famous speech in the history of the world was delivered, the spot where Jesus outlined the character and conduct of a believer and gave his disciples and the world the beatitudes, the golden rule, and the Lord's Prayer."

Bush relates an incident in which one of the group with "his friend, a Jew" had held hands underwater in the Sea of Galilee and prayed together:

> Then out of his mouth came a hymn he had known as a child, a hymn he hadn't thought about in years. He got every word right:
> *Now is the time approaching, by prophets long foretold, when all shall dwell together, One Shepherd and one fold. Now Jew and gentile, meeting, from many a distant shore, around an altar kneeling, one common Lord adore.*[40]

Bush's transcription of a hymn inspired by Darbyist dispensationalism concludes the only discussion of the Middle East in the book. In his account of his trip to Israel, Bush does not mention the Israeli citizens who are Arabs, the three million Arabs living under martial law curfews in the occupied territories, or the existence of Islam and the Muslim world, only "Jew and gentile." He treats Jewish history as nothing more than the prelude to, and the Holy Land as the stage for, the first coming of the incarnate God who saved his soul, Jesus Christ. There is every reason to assume that, like his fellow Texans Tom DeLay and Dick Armey, George W. Bush, converted to intense Protestant belief by Billy Graham, sincerely believes that God gave Abraham and his descendants the land of Israel—including Judea and Samaria—until the end of the world, just as it says in the Bible.

————————

The conservative imperialism of George W. Bush's administration has no precedents in U.S. foreign policy. But it has a striking resemblance to nineteenth-century British imperialism—a resemblance that grows even stronger when the traditional British/Southern nostrum of global free trade is added to the mix. Like nineteenth-century Britain, the twenty-first-century United States would police the world in "splendid isolation," promote free trade, and even foster the return of Jews to the Holy Land, a project of British evangelical Protestants in the nineteenth and early twentieth centuries and of American Protestant evangelicals in the late twentieth and twenty-first centuries.

In the nineteenth-century United States, the British imperialists found their closest political and economic allies among Americans in the Southern planter class. Most Southern planters, content for the United States to be a politically independent but economically dependent agricultural resource colony of the British Empire, opposed nationalists like Alexander Hamilton, Henry Clay, and Abraham Lincoln, who wanted to jump-start American industries by blocking British manufactured imports with high tariffs.

The fact that the twenty-first-century Southern conservative vision of a Pax Americana resembles the post-1945 Rooseveltian world order far less than it resembles the nineteenth-century British imperial world order, down to the fervent support of the state of Israel (a creation of the British Empire), is unsurprising. The South has always been, and remains, the most British part of the United States. Untouched, until recently, by non-British white immigration, the South, including Texas, is a provincial museum of dead British ideologies, British denominations, and British customs. The South's religion is seventeenth-century British Cromwellian Puritanism, as modified by nineteenth-century British Darbyist dispensationalism. The South's notion of social hierarchy is that of the eighteenth-century British landed elite, and its economic theory is that of nineteenth-century British free traders.

Having failed between 1861 and 1865 to escape from the United States in order to create their own militaristic, low-tariff, devoutly Protestant empire in the Caribbean and Central America, a Confederate empire that would have been allied with the global British Empire, conservative Southerners now seek to use the power of the U.S. presidency to remake the world in the image of the British Empire in the era of Queen Victoria—and of Jefferson Davis. The fact that, in order to do so, they have to repudiate half a century of Franklin Roosevelt's liberal internationalism, bothers them no more than the fact that the goal of global free trade requires them to repudiate the economic nationalism of Abraham Lincoln and his Republican successors. After all, as any Confederate patriot will tell you, Franklin Roosevelt and Abraham Lincoln were enemies of the South.

SEVEN

A Choice of Traditions

Texas, which many Texans and some outsiders like to think of as a nation-within-a-nation, is really two countries. The Lone Star State is a compound of two traditions, entwined in conflict, inside a single set of borders—and sometimes inside a single family or a single individual.

One Texas is the Texas of conservatives like George W. Bush and his predecessors: a society with a primitive economy based on agriculture, livestock, petroleum, and mining, with a poorly educated population of workers lacking health protection and job safety. In this Texas, low wages and inadequate spending on public goods like education and pollution abatement are considered a source of comparative economic advantage. This Texas is a toxic by-product of the hierarchical plantation society of the American South, a cruel caste society in which the white, brown, and black majority labor for inadequate rewards while a cultivated but callous oligarchy of rich white families and their hirelings in the professions dominate the economy, politics, and the rarefied air of academic and museum culture. The elite tends to be worldly and aristocratic in its attitudes, the working-class majority religious and fundamentalist; both the elite and the majority in this Texas share a profound social conservatism and an attachment to military values unknown anywhere else in the English-speaking world, except in other Southern states. The inhabitants of this Texas are deeply localist and tend to view Washington, D.C., as the enemy.

The other Texas is the Texas of Lyndon Johnson, Bobby Ray Inman, Ross Perot, Sam Rayburn, Wright Patman, Alvin Wirtz, and others in the modernist tradition. This Texas is a society eager to embrace the Space Age and the Information Age. The wealth of this Texas is based on the knowledge embodied in science and technology and disseminated by education. This Texas is led, not by good-old-boy businessmen and political demagogues, but by a visionary and earnest elite of entrepreneurs, engineers, reformist politicians, and dedicated civil servants, many of them self-made men and women from humble origins, often with backgrounds in the military. The economy of this Texas is radically different from that of the other Texas. It is a high-tech state-capitalist economy, in which government, business, and universities collaborate to promote innovation in computer science, biotech, and other cutting-edge fields, and in which public institutions supply needed investment capital, and expertise in the absence of a native, world-class entrepreneurial bourgeoisie. The leaders of this Texas usually share the pro-military ethic of their rivals and indeed are more likely than the oligarchs and their hirelings, the demagogues, to have served in the military. But the preferred society of these Texans is a broadly egalitarian meritocracy, not a traditional social order stratified by caste and class. Even if they are exclusively of Southern descent, they have little if any sense of Southern identity and no loyalty to the South as a region. They are sentimental nationalists for whom Texan patriotism is wholly fused with American patriotism. They believe that an activist federal government, when it is in the right hands, is an important ally of ordinary Texans.

The deepest political divide in Texas, as this book has explained, is not between "left" and "right," but between the oligarchic commodity-sector elite and the meritocratic elite of the state-capitalist tech sector—between the old "Saudi" Texas and the new "Japanese" Texas. The civil war between Saudi Texas and Japanese Texas explains the epic struggle between the Bush dynasty and Ross Perot in 1992, when Perot's run for president may have cost the senior Bush the White House. The Bush family symbolized oil wells and cheap labor on farms and ranches; Perot, computers and air-conditioned office parks. To Perot, the high-tech populist, the Bushes were upper-class parasites enriching themselves through the exploitation of natural resources that should have benefited all Texans. George Bush, Sr.,

siphoned oil out of the ground in Texas to pay for a country house in
Kennebunkport, Maine. Like an eighteenth-century British Caribbean
plantation owner residing in London, the elder Bush preferred not to
live in the barbaric place that provided him with his fortune. Perot
hated the Bushes and the Bakers the way that Juan Peron, another
modernizing tribune of the masses with a military background, once
hated the Anglophile oligarchs of the Buenos Aires Jockey Club.

These two states of Texas represent two traditions—the Texan
conservative tradition defined by the Old South and the Texan modernist tradition associated with the New Deal. For generations there
has been a civil war between these rival Texan traditions, and the conflict continues today. The outcome of this struggle has implications
not only for the state of Texas, but for the United States and the world
as a whole.

My argument in this book can be simply summarized. The industrial
and economic modernization of Texas, the South, and the United
States as a whole has been warped repeatedly by the Southern oligarchy. The Southern ruling class is not, and never has been, bourgeois. The wealthy families who for centuries have dominated politics
and the economy in the South, from Virginia to Texas, have roots in
Britain, not among the civic burghers but among the rural aristocracy.
The "cavaliers" are the heirs of medieval knights, not medieval merchants. Moving to the western hemisphere in the seventeenth and
eighteenth centuries, these British aristocrats and their upwardly
mobile imitators, on the slave plantations of the West Indies and the
North American mainland, created feudal systems without the recip-
rocal obligations to the rest of the society which, at least in theory,
moderated the rapacity of feudal European aristocracies. These
British-American planters, and their Spanish- and Portuguese- and
French-speaking equivalents in the western hemisphere, specialized
in exploiting slave labor in the export of crops and raw materials to
Western Europe.

Three times since 1776 the Southern oligarchy has distorted
America's economic and social progress. Following the establishment

of the United States, the Southern planters seized power in the federal government with the election of Thomas Jefferson in 1800. In the first half of the nineteenth century, the Southern oligarchs used their influence in the federal government to promote a low-tariff, free-trade regime that kept the United States stuck in the role of an informal agrarian resource colony of the British Empire. When the rise of the Republican Party in the 1850s threatened Southern control of Washington, D.C., the selfish planters tried to break away from the United States in order to form a Confederate slave-labor empire in the Caribbean and Central America.

The Confederate oligarchs lost the Civil War but won the battle of Reconstruction. In the 1870s, the Southern ruling class cut a deal with the Northern industrialists; the Southern oligarchy would be given a free hand to repress both Southern blacks and poor white Southerners, and to crush all political parties other than the Democrats, in return for exporting farm goods and raw materials to the factories of the Northeast and Midwest. Once again, the industrialization of the United States was warped by the South, which, along with its allies among Northeastern investors, had no interest in the diffusion of manufacturing outside of the industrial Northeast.

The industrial modernization of the South, which should have taken place after the Civil War, instead took place during the New Deal era, between 1932 and 1968. During the Depression, the Southern oligarchy, desperate for federal financial aid, joined opportunistically with Southern populists and liberals in supporting Franklin Roosevelt's policy of industrializing the South and West by means of state-capitalist projects like the TVA and the LCRA in Texas. But in the late 1930s, when the New Deal began to threaten the aristocratic, white-supremacist social order of the South, the Southern conservatives broke with Roosevelt and his Southern disciples like Lyndon Johnson. The Southern right used New Deal infrastructure projects to undermine the other economic reforms of the New Deal liberals, luring industries to the South with the promise of cheap labor, weak unions, and ineffective environmental laws.

Johnson's civil rights legislation of the 1960s was the final provocation for most Southern conservative Democrats; between the 1960s and the 1990s, waves of Southern "Dixiecrats" deserted the Democratic Party and joined the Republican Party. By the 1990s, ex-Democrats like Texas Senator Phil Gramm, a reactionary demagogue of the Old South school, controlled the GOP. The heirs of Jefferson Davis, having seized control of the party of Abraham Lincoln, used it to carry out what can be described, with little exaggeration, as two Southern coups d'etat. The attempted impeachment of President Bill Clinton, a Southern progressive, was led by reactionary Southern congressmen and opposed by most Americans other than white Southerners. The election of George W. Bush was viewed in many quarters as a successful Southern coup; having lost the majority vote, with his electoral vote tally in dispute, Bush was installed as a result of a vote by a majority of Supreme Court justices to end the Florida recount process. The vote in the Supreme Court split along ideological lines and regional lines, pitting Southwestern conservatives like Rehnquist and O'Connor against Northeasterners. Even supporters of the Supreme Court's action tended to agree that it was not justifiable in terms of constitutional law.

Installed in a lawless manner by the dominant Southern and Western conservative faction of the Supreme Court, George W. Bush, the candidate opposed by most American voters in the election of 2000, used the power of the presidency to promote the economic and foreign policy of agenda of the Southern far right: a massive tax cut as the centerpiece of domestic policy, and, in foreign policy, Protestant-fundamentalist-inspired support for the Likud Party of Israel, combined with consideration of schemes for an American takeover of the Iraqi and Saudi oil fields. From its conception of economics in terms of the exploitation of cheap labor and the plundering of non-renewable natural resources and its plan to replace the modern social safety net with "faith-based" religious charity, to its minimal-government political theory, its bellicose militarism, and its Bible Belt Christian Zionism, the second Bush administration illustrates the centuries-old traditions of the Southern oligarchy, of which the traditional Texan elite is a regional variant.

Today's Southern right combines the political economy of plantation owners with the fundamentalist religion of hillbillies. In the